Rosa,

Yes in the fac...

Peter Allen

# Life In The
# Fast Lane

# MISSION STATEMENT

Changing Lanes International is devoted to empowering 54,321 committed Lane Changers to navigate their road to success by accelerating their Recognition, AUTHORity and Collaborative Contribution to drive the world forward by 2030.

Printed in the United States of America

Life In The Fast Lane, December 2016

ISBN-13: 978-1541056596

ISBN-10: 1541056590

Changing Lanes International

www.changinglanesinternational.com

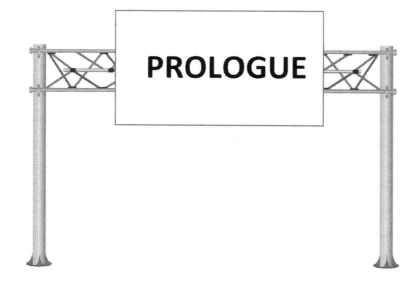

# PROLOGUE

There comes a moment in each of our lives when we realize if we are not where we want to be in life, it is time for a Lane Change. The road to success is paved with many who have started and stopped, only to give up when the journey proved tough. Does your future seem unclear and the indefinite obscurity halts any forward movement in your life? Remember, headlights do not show us the entire journey, but illuminate simply what is right in front of us. This allows us to continue moving forward enough to make forward progress towards our destination. The same concept applies to life. The point is not to know the future, but to be focused and aware enough to advance without swerving off the road.

The future to most is uncertain and full of ambiguous twists and turns. For Lane Changers, the future is where dreams are made. The reality is that your journey may seem overwhelming and daunting at times, but successful people continue pushing ahead despite not having all the answers. As a matter of fact, all accomplished experts and leaders make quick decisions and figure it out along the way. Life provides never-ending opportunities and those who seize those moments when they arise are the ones who get in to the fast lane. The road to success is always under construction and you may feel like pot holes keep popping up everywhere you turn. When we shift our mindset and shift gears to create our lives rather than letting life create our reality, we accelerate the process to pave an unsurpassed future.

When you go the extra mile, there is less competition. When you discover your greatest lane, there is no traffic. Lane Changers have the opportunity to use the carpool lane on the road to success. Our tribe rides together and our mentors help ease the strain of congestion along the way. We merge your purpose and passion with their skills and strategies. The purpose of this compilation is to give you a proverbial EZ pass so you do not have to run into some of the detours these experts did along the way. Moreover, a driver's manual provides valuable information when you need it; this book will serve as a guide to discover what successful leaders do and how they drive the world forward. We all have different vehicles – methods and avenues for creating success - but we are all on the road of life together. Lane Changers always take the high road.

The path to success is paved not just with good intentions but ethical values, hard work, patience, focus and massive action. It is your turn to say yes and trust the journey. It is your turn to make a shift and take your life into overdrive. It is time to put the pedal to the metal. Do not let life pass you by. Bypass the good life on the way to your best life. Make a shift and take your life into overdrive. It is time to accelerate your dreams. Now is the ideal time to live 'Life in the Fast Lane.' Are you ready to take the wheel?

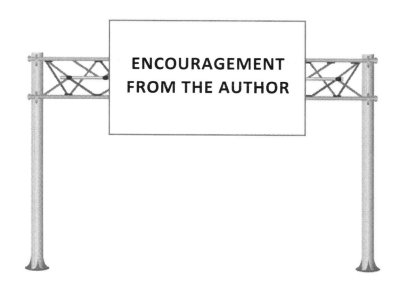

## ENCOURAGEMENT FROM THE AUTHOR

Should you turn left, because nothing is going right? Or should you turn right, because you have nothing left? Life and business can feel like one big traffic jam - we have to battle stress, the challenges of building a business, the haters who doubt us along the way, "back seat drivers" who think they know better than us what we should be doing with our lives, self-doubt, constant setbacks, and perpetual roadblocks that prevent us from a smooth ride toward greatness.

Life is highway full of potholes, bumps, detours, and alternate routes. It is your choice to make the turn that leads you to your destiny. In due course, the fears we do not face become our limits. Lane Changers know the greater the change, the greater the joy. A road map gives us freedom to travel as we wish. A set of directions gives us the best route to get where we desire. In the end, it is not the places we have been that matter, but those we have yet to experience that determine our destiny. Success in life comes at the intersection of passion and massive action. When it comes to choosing a lane, most take a back seat to what they truly want and settle for what they accept, which is far less than their ultimate capability.

Perhaps it is time to buckle up and drive forward toward your true potential. We may not always see the ultimate destination, but when we keep on trucking, we can change lanes and change the course of our lives, and millions of others along the way. This is your turn. Your destination matters. You must be willing to take the wheel. Be bold on the boulevard of your dreams. Aspire to take the avenue that is best for you. Take the lane that makes you the greatest leader. Reflect on the expedition of the road that has led you where you are now. As you read each chapter from individual 'drivers' who have created massive success in their own lives, ask yourself: "How 'concrete' is my road to success?"

The driver who has already been there has valuable hindsight that could serve as your foresight. Their rearview mirror becomes your windshield. Possibly, when you finish the book, if nothing else, you look in the rear view mirror and acknowledge where you've been, is not where you want to keep going. The world is an open highway. Each of these contributors chose to take the fast lane. It may not be a road you would follow. But perhaps, just by chance, your roads cross and you can drive the world forward together. On the road to our greatest life, the destination we are seeking is only achieved by maximizing our capacity to give and contribute. In the end, when you combine your best attitude with your best aptitude, you will get into the fast lane. You hold the wheel that will direct your ultimate destiny.

Direction ultimately becomes more important than speed. Many are going nowhere fast. Some people are on the right track, going the wrong way. Others are on the wrong track, going the right way. It is time to get on the right track going the right way. The best thing in life is knowing that no matter how hard the road may get, everyone can reach their own destination in their own time. This book will ensure you are not one of the many people going nowhere recklessly! On the road of life, everything you construct starts in your mind. Make sure you remain in alignment with your core values. There will always be a high road and a low road. Few do whatever it takes to get on the high road and stay there. Go the extra mile; most people exit before then so it is a wide open road to success.

Are you ready to take the wheel and become who you want rather than who you almost could have been? This book is designed to serve as a driver's manual to help you get a tune up, to course correct where necessary for your journey, to make the essential adjustments, and if needed, to make an entire Lane Change. This is just the beginning. Take the principles and guidelines from the stories and implement them immediately. That, friends, is where the rubber meets the road.

Drive the world forward,

Lane Ethridge

Founder & CEO of Changing Lanes International

## HER HEART IS IN THE RIGHT PLACE

*"Yesterday is history. Tomorrow is a mystery.*
*Today is a gift, that's why they call it the present."*
*~ Bil Keane*

# Alyssa Sandeen

Many times throughout life we feel like someone is holding our heart in the palm of their hands. Our hearts are the central focus of love and passion and when two people are connected it is because their hearts yearn for one another. When life is challenging and we face our darkest days, it can feel like our heart is being ripped out of our chest. Yet, many of us will never actually experience having our heart removed physically from our bodies. Certainly, most of us will never have that experience twice, like Alyssa Sandeen.

At 8 years old, when most kids are excited about going to school and visiting their friends, Alyssa was visiting hospitals. While siblings are fighting for the remote to their video game systems, Alyssa was fighting for her life. Raised in Mankato, a small quaint town along a large bend of the Minnesota river, it is certainly a community where the people are as nice as the rolling hills covering the vast acreage of God's country. Alyssa dreamed of hunting and spending her time outdoors; unfortunately, her childhood was spent indoors. Rather than hunting for wild game, her organs were the ones being targeted in the wild game of life.

One day when Alyssa was 8 years old, she began complaining about not feeling well. Her mother, Lisa, took her to the doctor where she was diagnosed with flu-like symptoms. During a family vacation in the Twin-cities, her symptoms continued to persist and her mom took her in for another checkup, a day that would begin a long and treacherous stretch of hospital visits. While at Minneapolis Hospital, despite the doctor releasing her, the nurses encouraged the doctor to admit her overnight, a commendation that most likely saved her life, and not just the first time.

She was admitted to Children's Hospital where the nurses recognized the severity of the complications. Much to her parent's disapproval, her nurses encouraged them to do a biopsy that had never been done before. Alyssa was airlifted to Rochester St. Mary's Hospital where she was put on a heart-lung machine and life support with a recommended 7-day maximum, yet she remained on it for eleven. As she awoke the next morning, given less than 5% chance of living, a priest read her last rights to the family. Completely sedated, nearly incapable of moving physically, upon hearing the priest's proclamation, Alyssa's body miraculously sat up, something a priest had never seen before. By sitting up, Alyssa was standing up for herself and her life.

Alyssa, who's life literally hung in the balance, hung onto the hope that she would be given new life. Her vitals were failing and she received the ultimate opportunity to fight for her life at the blessing from an angel on Earth. Her new heart was donated from a 5-year old boy, Matthew, who was an only child, after he had been hit by a truck. Unbeknownst to BJ, the mother of the 5-year old boy whose heart was inside Alyssa's chest, she had the opportunity to meet Alyssa and her parents on the John Walsh Show 5 years after the transplant. This moment drove Alyssa to unconditional appreciation. Matthew, which means a gift from God, had literally offered the gift of life to Alyssa.

"She deserved to live so much. She enjoys life more than anybody and I'm so happy for her," Alyssa's father, Chris decrees. "We are so grateful to Alyssa's heart donor's family. Without them, Alyssa wouldn't be here. She's so full of life; her goal is always to make people smile and make them happy."

Throughout life each of us experiences moments in our lives that change everything. When we feel like we can't take one more step, we put one foot in front of the other anyway. When we feel like we can't make one more sales call, we pick up the phone and dial that prospect anyway. When we feel like we can't pay our bills because of insufficient funds, we find a way to make enough to keep the lights on. When we experience these moments, the ones where we 'cross our heart and hope to die,', perhaps we reflect on the fact that many of us will not know the feeling of barely being able to take one more breath, one that may breathe new life to literally survive.

Life is a constant battle to thrive and yet Alyssa, each day of her childhood had to fight to survive. Perhaps the things we take for granted are not such luxuries for others.  When we experience trial after trial, we must fight hard enough and long enough to turn those trials into a triumphs. Due to her constant health struggles creating an "abnormal" lifestyle for an 8-year old, Alyssa was home-schooled until high school where she got to experience a "normal" life. But not for long.

In 2010, as a result of the many medications, her kidney started to deteriorate. Visiting the doctor again, he recommended dialysis immediately. Alyssa's mom, healthy her entire life, was a perfect match and became her donor. They went into the operation together and after a successful procedure, were designated to different floors. Alyssa was so elated and felt amazing but her mom had negative symptoms and was really sick post-operation. During the first night after the procedure, Alyssa wanted to see her mom and snuck out of her room, into a private elevator, down to Lisa's room. Hugging her, Alyssa's name was called over the loud speaker demanding her back to her room. Mother and child, joined forever by their love, were now connected physically, and while their bodies were recovering, they both embodied strength and courage together.

Throughout her visitations, God had His hand on the timing and location of each. While there isn't much in Mankato, it sits nearby some of the most acclaimed hospitals and medical facilities which became not only a temporary home, but a house of worship and prayer for Alyssa. One year after her kidney transplant, this time in the emergency room, Alyssa flat lined. A floating nurse, who had never performed CPR was able to revive her. Back on life support for a month, she was able to recover. The entire experience happened again one year later. Alyssa flat lined for 2 ½ hours. Nurses patiently and courageously continued CPR the entire time. Why they didn't give up after 30 minutes Alyssa cannot comprehend, but is eternally grateful and appreciative for each of their efforts. Considering many of them had to go to therapy because of the traumatic experience, those nurses will forever know they literally saved a life that day.

But it wasn't met with simplicity. Nothing in Alyssa's life to this point was unpretentious. During the immaculate revival, a needle caused her central line to burst which caused her entire chest to burn. For the third time she went on life support, this time losing oxygen blood flow. This forced the doctors to save her major organs like her brain and heart, and created an 80% chance of losing her leg. "Mom and dad you need to get this out there. You need to get as many people praying as possible. I'm young, I don't want to lose my leg on top of everything else that has happened," Alyssa implored. Through a successful fasciotomy to get rid of the blood clot, along with lots of prayer, her leg was saved. Like a hunter, she was focused, but in the game of life with her uncertain health, she wasn't out of the woods yet. Her heart was now again the target.

For the next 3 months, Alyssa waited for a matching heart to get a transplant. Due to getting sick of being in hospitals, she wanted to be at home while she waited. Day by day, not knowing when or even if she would receive a heart, she experienced emotional and physical pain. Every other day she would go to Rochester, a nearby city, to be treated for burn therapy. Her body, depleted and vulnerable, contracted pneumonia. During one of her visits, she had a heart attack and because a patient moves higher on the donor list if he or she is living in the hospital, Alyssa was readmitted.

Completely immobile, on top of waiting for her heart, Alyssa continued to have excruciating pain forcing her to uncontrollably sob at least 8 times a day. During physical therapy, if she was able to move her big toe it was a large success. While it wasn't a life-changing improvement, it provided hope that she could continue to progress. Small disappointments add up over time. So do small successes. The ones you focus on more will multiply your results. "I thought each time I was intubated in the ICU this was it. I'm gone. I can't do this anymore. Every single day is basically like living in Hell. Somehow, I knew I wouldn't give up," she discloses.

Alyssa, despite her living Hell, knew that Heaven was a better place but her Heaven on Earth was hunting and fishing. She would order cowboy boots just to give her a vision that one day, despite not even able to move her big toe, she would be able to walk in them. When we feel like we can't take one more step, we put one foot in front of the other anyway. As Alyssa was nearly at wit's end, there was a glimmer of hope. Her nurse told her she couldn't eat anymore because she was due for an upcoming surgery. Could it be? Was there a chance she would be getting out? Her heart beat faster thinking about her new heart. Blessed again with a donor, this time a 21-year old female, Alyssa was given another fighting chance.

We are all dealt a hand in life; we cannot change the cards we are dealt, just the we play the cards determines our fortune. Alyssa has been handed many opportunities to continue living her legacy. We may not have been dealt the greatest hand in life, but the worst thing we can do is permanently fold on life. Many want an Ace up their sleeve - Alyssa is lucky she got 3 total hearts and gets to wear her heart on her sleeve every day. On the road of life there are many lane changes, some of which result in a dead end for some and for some a new avenue to live. For Alyssa, getting into the fast lane wasn't as important as being in a car for the first time on the way home with her new heart providing life abundantly.

While we may not ever experience a mere glimpse of Alyssa's conditions, perhaps the best Lane Change we can ever make is having a change of heart overall - the way we perceive life and the way we respond to the things that happen to us are more important than the things that happen to us. Alyssa acknowledges "I never thought I would be able to be here to talk about my success story. I'm taking good care of it and will continue to take good care of my heart. I wouldn't be able to help others out if they didn't help me out."

Throughout the roller coaster journey for Alyssa, she recognizes that even though she was on her death bed and was living a nightmare on it, she continued to dream. She also recognized and reminded herself there are people who have it worse all around the world. While she struggled to survive, she at least had access to food and drugs that could help her. Her family was such a huge support system and she concedes that without them she wouldn't have had the strength to keep fighting. Often, our family or community become the foundation on which we can lean. Due to their prayers and encouragement, Alyssa was ultimately victorious.

Faith also played a tremendous part in her ability to prevail. Faith that begins with fear brings you closer to joy. One of her goals, like being able to move her big toe, was to attend church every Sunday. Even when we can't stand, we can kneel. Her organs have been through Hell but the organs of Heaven play majestically because of Alyssa, another angel on Earth. Alyssa, a dancer her whole life when able, has angels in Heaven dancing in jubilation.

"I want people to know it's all good but it's not always going to be smooth sailing. You can get through it," Alyssa proclaims. "Because of my journey, I have realistic goals that are unrealistic to other people. I was scared to death of dying so early. I haven't lived my life yet," she believes. Our setbacks set us up for a comeback. Life can always be worse and life could always be better. When life takes you down a dark road, remember Alyssa and don't lose heart (she's already done that for you twice). The moment we have before us is the most precious. We all have a first chance but not all of us get a second chance. And it's a miracle Alyssa got a second chance. What are you holding back from taking a chance on to improve your life? When is the LAST time you did something for the FIRST time? Is it possible TODAY you will do a first and don't realize it will be your last? You don't live life, you create it.

Life as many lifetimes as you can before your life comes to the final dead end. Sometimes it's best to be in the fast lane and sometimes it's a gift just to be alive to be driving the world forward at all. It is your turn. There are many people on life support and you may be the one who could support a life. Having a heart for someone takes a whole new meaning. Who can you open your heart to today to make their life better?

Perhaps it's time for each of us look at our hearts and see if they are truly beating for what our hearts break for. When we follow that road it will lead us to the greatest fulfillment and the ability to create our biggest contribution.

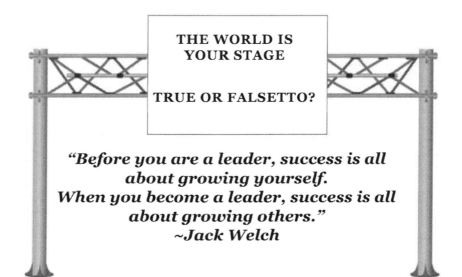

THE WORLD IS
YOUR STAGE

TRUE OR FALSETTO?

*"Before you are a leader, success is all about growing yourself. When you become a leader, success is all about growing others."*
*~Jack Welch*

# Betsy-Allen Manning

We all have a turning point in life where we decide that we must turn our back on those who don't believe in us, and turn toward our dreams and toward those who encourage us. The road to each level of success is paved with various difficulties. And yet smooth roads do not create skillful drivers. Often, the best thing you can do is roll the windows down and turn the radio up; or better yet, sing your own song on the journey to your greatest life.

Betsy Allen-Manning knew she wanted to be a singer from age 3. She would lock herself in the bathroom, singing for hours while standing on top of the toilet seat because the acoustics were better the higher you got. As she grew older, her desire to be a singer grew more real. She had friends who were headliners on cruise ships and Betsy realized there would be nothing better than getting paid to travel the world and do what she loves!

Auditioning in Chicago at age 19 for a position as a headliner on a cruise ship, she discovered the higher she got, the harder her critics got. After her performance for the audition, receiving mostly praise from the judges, she also received feedback from the vocal coach, a former Broadway star. Her evaluation would change everything. "Betsy," she said, "when our headliners get done singing, they command a standing ovation because they're that good. You would have been lucky to get a handshake for that pathetic performance you just gave. If your goal is to be a headliner you might as well just quit now because you don't have what it takes and you probably never will."

Heartbroken, Betsy thanked them and went up to her hotel room, crying. She called her mom hoping for condolences and protection, but instead got even more than she wanted. "Betsy," her mom inquired fairly bluntly, "Are you good enough to be the headliner right now?" Betsy replied, "No, honestly I am not right now."

"Well do you think you can be?" her mom delved.

"I know I can be," Betsy confidently remarked.

Her mom encouraged her to take the job they offered as a backup singer-dancer and hire one of the headliners on the cruise ship to coach her. "Take some of that money and invest it into your future success," she remembers her mom encouraging her. Betsy discovered that people who don't want the best for you will tell you what you want to hear. Mentors, those who truly want you to succeed, will tell you what you need to hear. She also understood the importance of investing in herself in order to eventually have her dreams ring true.

When you have clarity about your purpose in life, you must work on your skills. Just because you want it does not mean you're equipped with the skills to excel. With improved abilities, comes improved confidence to execute the job. While Betsy started her love of singing in the bathroom, she didn't want to see her dreams go down the toilet. She hired the headliner on the cruise ship, created a game plan and diligently worked on her skills.

A year and a half later, she auditioned on another cruise ship as a backup singer-dancer. When she finished, the judge asked her why she didn't apply to be the headliner, acknowledging she had all the competences of a headliner. Never settle for what you believe you're capable of; instead strive for what you don't even know you're capable of.

After her first live, solo performance in front of 1200 people, as she ended her show and controlled the stage, the crowd rising to their feet for her first standing ovation, with a tear strolling down her face, Betsy had proven to herself she had what it takes. While she was ecstatic, what she remembers about that night wasn't just the experience, but the impact it made.

One of her singer-dancers asked if Betsy would coach her. Betsy had gone from being a mentee to a mentor, and her heart truly sang in that moment. Great leaders don't wait for the opportunity to lead, they lead and then they're presented with opportunities. She realized that her purpose was not just to fulfill her own dreams, but when you reach a certain level of success in your own life, doors open and the true reward in life comes from helping others reach their own success. For the next twelve years, Betsy got paid to travel the world and live out her dream.

Through her journey, Betsy discovered when you think you've grown and think you've learned everything, that's when you start falling down. Focus, discipline and consistent action will help you get into the fast lane. The more you work on your skill set the more you must also work on your mindset. And above each of those, you must continually build your character. When you think you've arrived, stretch yourself and do something new. When you take a leap of faith, God will bless you with an experience that you wouldn't even imagine possible. Sometimes it simply takes having the heart to be willing to start.

And the same way doors will open, doors will also close in order to lead you to new opportunities. Lane changes are God's way of giving you a new chance to discover more about yourself and go in a new direction. Betsy eventually developed a strain on her vocal cords and she lost her upper range, losing the ability to sing. When you lose your capacity to do what you love most, there is a period emptiness. There are seasons of life where it's acceptable to grieve and cherish the journey you were on. And yet, since we cannot remain complacent, when it's time to move on you must take action to create a new life.

Betsy made a shift from serving her purpose to serving others. As a cocktail waitress in Vegas, a position where her management was driven by fear and punishment, she learned a lot about what didn't work in leadership. As she moved up to higher management positions, she began adopting their mentality and culture, but it just didn't feel right. She wanted to move on but didn't know what to do. Her dad, giving her advice, suggested that "You're only stuck if you want to be stuck." Betsy questioned her ability to be a leader and considered perhaps she wasn't cut out for management. "That's the easy road out," her dad reminded her. Self-discovery is always more powerful than a truth told.

Betsy realized that she would always take the high road. She made it her mission to always be the best leader she could be. She invested in herself again because with each avenue we pursue there are different skills we need. She read "How to Win Friends and Influence People" by Dale Carnegie. She became a member of the John Maxwell team because he was the #1 expert in the world on leadership and if you want to be the best you have to learn from the best. She became DISC certified and became a human behavior specialist in order to understand people better. She was reminded the same way as a singer that great leaders don't wait for the opportunity to lead, they lead and then they're given opportunities.

Betsy eventually went on to be a hiring manager and develop the training program for a new $70 million venue at one of the most prominent hotels in Vegas. Betsy became proficient at taking information and turning it into application. Every time she learns something, she figures how to apply the information one of three ways:

- Where can I use this information?
- When can I use this information?
- Who can I share this information with?

She learned through her success in going to new levels that what separates successful people from average people is being a '100%-er.' It's just as important to give 100% to the things you love and equally, you must give 100% to the things you loathe.

Betsy, at least from a cultural standpoint, had everything - money, a house and cars, an amazing family and a phenomenal group of friends. Working 16 hours a day, however, she didn't have time to enjoy her success. She felt called to a higher purpose, to do more with her life. On a two-week trip to Italy, she continued to listen to her intuition. Upon returning home, with nothing else lined up, she gave her notice of resignation. Through a partnership with a person who wasn't the right fit for her company, Betsy lost everything. The importance of aligning with someone who has similar morals and values became significantly more apparent to her.

When you have to start from scratch, you have to scratch your plans and surrender to your higher purpose. Betsy had always created a game plan for her life and this time, she was willing to follow God's plan for her life. She was reminded that the 'heart of man plans his way, but the Lord establishes his steps.' Do you go left when nothing's right or do you go right when you have nothing left?

Throughout life we experience seasons where you will thrive and there are others where you just need to survive. The road as an entrepreneur is paved with uncertainty. Betsy recognized that you can't let your circumstances control you because you always have the ability to take control of your emotions in any circumstance. There are some people who are driving toward their goals and dreams. There are also people driving aimlessly hoping to find their purpose and ultimately their desired destination. And throughout the road of life, there will be times where you experience both. Coaches and mentors will become your GPS – They'll help you create your Goals. They'll help you create a Plan. And then you will Succeed

Do not let anybody tell you that you don't have what it takes. There are those who will tell us that we can, and those who will tell us that we cannot. But ultimately, you must have a fight within you and the unwavering determination to succeed. Always be the best version of yourself and if you don't believe you are at this point, continue working on your craft and make it a point to become that version of yourself. You may not see all the rewards you will receive along the journey. You don't have to. You just need to show up and blessings will surely follow. Everything will reveal itself when you start to pursue your purpose.

Betsy followed the tug on her heart and continued to pursue her higher purpose as a motivational speaker.

She began making videos and taking the necessary steps. Eventually she was offered a nationwide speaking tour. She was back on the road, following her God-given desire to affect lives, again through her voice. Through traveling and sharing her gift, she was led to the greatest, unexpected gift in her life. Through the roadblocks, speed bumps and tolls in Betsy's life, God used the broken road she was on to lead her to her husband, and a career she loves.

Take a chance to make a change. If you're not willing to invest in your future than you can't complain about where you are now.

You may not want to be the next American Idol, but whatever you want to accomplish, don't sit idle. We all have a song to sing. We all have a voice. And when you become a 100%-er, you will be able to fulfill one of the greatest songs ever recorded, and truly live "Life in the Fast Lane."

# THE GOLDEN OPPORTUNITY

*"Now faith is confidence in what we hope for and assurance by what we do not see."*
*— Hebrews 11:1*

## Brenda Geary

Brenda Geary's infectious laugh and cheerful smile nearly disguise the tough adversities she has overcome but not the sincerity of her faith, her gratitude and her endlessly positive attitude. Her story is one of constant forward motion with "lane changes" that redefined her goals and led her through a series of tough challenges, a few heartbreaks and a string of accomplishments in the corporate world and in her personal life

Now 52, Brenda spent her childhood on Air Force bases, the second daughter in a family of five children. She was born in Puerto Rico to a single mom who had grown up in unrelenting poverty and had been determined to raise her daughters differently. Her mother met a young U.S. airman stationed in Puerto Rico, fell in love him and married him. He adopted Brenda and her sister and then her parents had two more daughters and a son.

The family lived in Puerto Rico until Brenda was 6 and then moved to the U.S. and traveled from base to base like many military families. On visits to her mother's family in Puerto Rico, Brenda experienced the poverty that her mother had grown up in: outhouses, dilapidated houses and more. But back in the states, her life was good as her stepfather continued in his Air Force career and her mother made a nice home for the five children. Because she saw poverty first hand, she appreciated the life her parents were giving her and later, as a mother, passed along those lessons of appreciation to her son.

Then everything changed when her mother began battling cancer. Her parents' relationship became strained. Alcohol, arguments and violence punctuated their once-happy household. Brenda and her sisters and brother became targets of their parents' struggle. But, beyond their four walls, Brenda saw other families and individuals in different situations. This gave her refuge and inspiration. She knew, like her mother before her, that there could be a better life. She spent a lot of time at her friends' homes. She learned to please others and to be the "good girl" to avoid the conflicts at home.

At school, her friends were preparing for college so she decided she would find a way to go to college also. In middle school, she babysat and delivered newspapers for money to buy the things she needed as the family budget was tight. Then as a teenager in Rantoul, Illinois, she took a job at a McDonald's restaurant and by the time she was old enough to go to college her job was providing enough money she could pay her college expenses at the University of Illinois. At the same time, the work experience at McDonald's taught her how to follow a system and how her hard work really would pay off. This became the foundation of the work ethic and focus on customer service that would serve her well later. Meanwhile, Jerry Minion, the McDonald's owner/operator, and John Thompson, the manager, took an interest in her and became early mentors who supported her, believed in her and even coached her while she worked for them and even after she moved on.

In her sophomore year, she fell in love and got married. A baby followed shortly. She took a semester off and then went back to working full-time at McDonald's and going to school full-time. By the end of her junior year, she came to the difficult realization that the marriage was over. It had not been the partnership of equals "until death do us part" that she had envisioned, and with the support of her friends, co-workers and her mother, she changed lanes, got a divorce and forged ahead with her commitment to her education and to be a single parent to Michael.

Her mother, who had quit school in the ninth grade to help support her family, didn't understand the academic challenges Brenda faced, but did provide loving care for Brenda's son Michael while Brenda studied and worked. At her graduation ceremony, amid the flurry of caps and gowns, the majestic music and noted speakers, her mother came to realize for the first time the scope of Brenda's academic success. She continued to be Brenda's biggest cheerleader for the rest of her life.

After graduation, Brenda thought she would go into management in the McDonald's organization and become a restaurant manager. But there was another lane change approaching and Brenda ended up pursing a different career route.

Earlier, she had been walking through a classroom building when she overheard a video discussing training and personnel development. She followed the sound of the video into an office that turned out to be the admissions office for the human resources management program at the U of I. She sat down and asked a woman behind a desk what it would take to become part of that degree program. She found out she was talking to the admissions director herself! The director spelled out the extensive requirements for admission and Brenda realized she would have a tough time passing the math section of the required graduate entrance exam. Determined to get into graduate school now, she tutored alongside teenagers in a math program for six months. She passed the math section of the entrance exam and was admitted. She even earned a grant that enabled her, for the first time, to attend school full-time and still take care of Michael. As a lane changer, she was willing to do whatever she had to do to achieve her goal.

For the next two years, Brenda attended school full-time and earned a Master's Degree in Human Resources Management. Her record as a top student with an unbelievable work ethic was a magnet to corporate recruiters. She had prepared well and the lanes opened up. She had her choice on the open road. She had interviews and on-site visits with top companies and looked closely at a Fortune Five company offering an entry into an executive leadership program. The program required four assignments in different locations, but she couldn't move Michael every six months now that he was in school. She said no, but the company changed lanes to bring this talented HR leader into their team and offered her two assignments in two towns. She took it.

Her first mentor told her: "You are either a minnow or a shark in this company. You need to decide which you are and by the way the minnows get eaten up by the sharks." Brenda learned to be assertive, to speak up and to work even harder. She would never be a minnow. As her corporate responsibilities grew, her mother came to live with her and Michael during her second assignment. By then a three-time cancer survivor, her mother developed another issue and died unexpectedly. Brenda lost her most sincere supporter.

See back of receipt for your chance
to win $1000

ID #:   7L2GNC1FG57V

# Walmart >'<

## Neighborhood Market

( 915 ) 206 - 6139
MANAGER ADRIANA RANGEL
101 E. REDD RD
EL PASO, TX 79932
ST# 04105 OP# 000411 TE# 02 TR# 07046
CILANTRO        000000004889KF       0.33 N
JALAPENOS       000000004693KF
  0.58 lb  @  1 lb /0.68            0.39 N
AVOCADO         000000004046KF
  4 AT  1 FOR    0.78               3.12 N
SPREADS         002740010307 F      2.00 0
OREO I/C CY     001626401105 F     14.98 0
CORONA  BEER    003354495042       14.98 T
M MS            004000050290 F      1.34 X
DS STYLISH      001101757005        7.97 X
FOIL            007874207676        2.76 X
                    SUBTOTAL       47.87
         TAX 1    8.250 %           2.23
                       TOTAL       50.10
                VISA  TEND         50.10
Visa Credit   **** **** **** 6170   I 1
APPROVAL # 00441B
REF # 1042000314
TRANS ID - 467284756801454
VALIDATION - M4JJ
PAYMENT SERVICE - E

AID A0000000031010
TC 9ABFBF3C9E6208BA
TERMINAL # SC011519
*Signature Verified

        10/11/17      15:01:46
               CHANGE DUE           0.00
        # ITEMS SOLD 12
     TC# 6/05 3721 54   4113 5713

Low Prices You Can Trust. Every Day.
        10/11/17      15:01:47
           ***CUSTOMER COPY***

Store receipts on your phone. Walmart P
ay.

As she dealt with the grief, she found new strength in friendships and relationships with trusted co-workers and others moving up the corporate ladder. With each new assignment, she overcame fear, trusted herself, developed new needed skills and sought out new mentors. For ten years she climbed the corporate ladder and achieved a top level of executive leadership. Within this large corporation, she moved from business to business, learning new products and services and constantly improving her skills as an HR professional. She became a mentor to younger employees and a seasoned adviser to leaders at the top. She helped them create high-performing teams that would outpace the competition.

She made sure everyone had the latest skills and the most up to date resources. She had the versatility to help two employees settle a seemingly petty disagreement while crafting long-range development strategies that enabled businesses to grow around the world. She recruited new employees and got them up to speed fast. She developed diversity plans that created a multi-layer workforce of brilliant minds who could solve problem and seize opportunities better and faster than the competition.

Then, during a particularly challenging assignment in Chicago, she couldn't shake a series of illnesses and instead of recovering grew sicker. She worked harder to catch up and then became sick again and again. Doctors diagnosed her with one issue after another, but never got to the root of the problem. She was sent to multiple hospitals and specialists who ran multiple tests to find the root of the problem, but the only thread of hope was around an array of autoimmune diagnoses without real solutions.

She took an assignment in San Diego thinking the sunnier weather would certainly help her recover. Instead, she grew even more ill and was diagnosed with chronic fatigue, fibromyalgia and severe allergies. She ached all over and was exhausted. On an important conference call, she realized she couldn't remember her boss' name, another side effect of these difficult issues. She knew she had to change lanes and leave her job to focus on rebuilding her health.

With new doctors and new treatments, she discovered she had been misdiagnosed in Chicago and that her recovery would take quite some time. As her health started to improve, she reached out to friends who had been important to her at different times in her life and her career. One was a man she dated in high school who she had considered her "first love." A simple "Google" search and she found a phone number for Randy Geary and left a message, thinking she would never hear back. Instead, Randy called her and they talked for seven hours straight, covering the last 22 years of their lives and deciding this time they would be together forever. Brenda's illness, and the side-effects 24 different prescription medications, had boosted her weight by 120 pounds. She warned Randy that the Brenda he remembered wouldn't be the Brenda he would see when they met, but Randy saw the "real" Brenda and a year later they were married.

A retired police officer, Randy's new occupation was taking care of Brenda. The two knew that true love is appreciating each other for who they are and unconditionally providing for them when they need you the most. Randy came into Brenda's life for love, but he also was an angel. While grabbing lunch one day at a McDonald's nearby, he sat down next to a young man who started up a conversation. Randy shared the fact that his wife was ill and the young man asked if Brenda and Randy would be open to watching an ABC Primetime investigative report that featured a product he was representing.

They watched the report and found a plan and a product that would help Brenda regain her health. As her health steadily improved, she continued to have regular check-ups and cancer screenings, knowing she and her sisters were at risk for cancer due to their mother's experience. After a routine mammogram, Brenda was asked to follow up with an ultrasound.  The day before Thanksgiving in 2011 Brenda found out she had breast cancer.

This lane change was a tough one. She thought she was on the road to recovery, but now the road was paved with chemotherapy and radiation. Randy was her champion. Old friends far away supported her mentally while new friends locally supported her with visits and advice. The treatments were tough and the roller coaster of emotions and energy in between were difficult. In the end she was cancer free and back on the road to recovery.

When she left the corporate world, she found a part of her identity left as well. She was a human resources leader, with no team to lead. In a way she felt guilty that she had left her purpose in life behind. She prayed about this feeling of purpose, asking God to guide her. Until she saw cancer herself, she didn't fully grasp its impact. Although she had experienced it second-hand with her mother three times, she didn't understand it fully until she experienced it herself. It was then that she realized her purpose in life was much more than her work in human resources. Her purpose was to help others and to inspire people with her story, her recovery and her journey through the ups and downs of life. She has a special place in her heart for people diagnosed with cancer. She provides hope for women around the world and women she meets around the corner.

When you put yourself last and let other people's problems or your co-workers goals overshadow you, you set yourself up to finish last. Instead, by putting yourself first you can build your health and wellness and help others along their journey by teaching them how to put themselves first.

Brenda believes that "when you don't have your health, you don't have anything". No amount of money can replace the loss of good health. Her strong beliefs in the importance of good health are what fuel her passion for educating people on health and wellness maintenance and disease prevention.

Brenda's nine-year journey of living with and then finding relief from chronic pain, auto immune issues and cancer is at the core of her passion for helping people who are suffering from similar issues. Brenda believes that because she has experienced so many health issues that she can relate directly to the challenges that others face. She knows what it's like to have pain that medication can't take away or to not have the strength or stamina to get out of bed. She has experienced the struggle of coping with depression related to being sick and feeling hopeless. The depression that one experiences when they see no light at the end of the tunnel related to chronic pain.

Brenda can understand the feeling of loss of self-esteem and confidence experienced going from being a high level corporate executive or a person fully functioning to suffering from chronic short term memory issues. She understands the heavy toll that chronic illness can have in a family. She saw it happen to her family when her mother fought cancer three times and then she saw the toll it took in her own family life.

Today Brenda is cancer free and has found a special calling for helping provide support to women that have been recently diagnosed with breast cancer, helping them navigate the fear and uncertainty of a new diagnosis. Being able to share as survivor what a newly diagnosed person might expect to encounter, she is often asked to speak and share her cancer story to support newly diagnosed women.

Brenda is embracing her new purpose in life. In true "lane changer" style she is excited about making a huge impact in the lives of others and fully embracing the journey and challenges.

Her belief is that if you want to accomplish something, there are no excuses but only end results. Brenda's success is based on her strong desire to win, her willingness to put in the work, her willingness to fail and get up again and most importantly in her ability to find mentors that have been able to guide her journey. When you put yourself last that's the place you'll end up; instead, touch a lot of lives along your road to greatness and you can put yourself first while helping others do the same. In this way, Brenda and Randy have become role models for others.

Sometimes we don't see what others do to create success; yet when we discover the lengths they went to get to where they are, we want to be around them and support them. So many people want to get in the fast lane and draft off the forward momentum of others. Brenda has always been a leader and now many people get to benefit from her consistent effort toward greatness. Brenda is living a life of genuine purpose and passion.

"If you want to lead the orchestra,
you must turn your back on the crowd."
~ Max Lucado

# Craig Duswalt

When the stars align our world becomes a galaxy of possibilities that allow our unique gifts to shift the entire universe. When rock stars align, the entire universe becomes their stage. For Craig Duswalt, the "RockStar Marketer," the world is his stage. Craig got his first job at the Westbury Music Fair in Long Island, NY as a runner back stage because he wanted to become an actor. He understood that surrounding himself with people in the industry was a great way to expose himself to opportunities. The lowest man on the totem pole, he knew he could climb.

With his first equity gig playing a small role in "The Sound of Music," Craig believed acting was his future. Even with all the bright lights shining upon him on stage, his future was about to get even brighter than he imagined. The popular Australian band, Air Supply, was doing a 2-night show at the venue and Craig was fortunate enough to be working the first show as the runner. With a ton of positive energy and a perpetual positive attitude, running around like a mad man, Craig excelled at his menial responsibilities and believes that when we give everything we have to anything we do, success is soon to follow.

His mother, a fan of the band, insisted that Craig take her to the show the second night. During the performance, assuming he had a relationship with the band, asserted that they go back stage to meet the band. Obliging, Craig took his mom back stage to meet them despite not really knowing them himself. A large man approached them and asked Craig if he was the guy working the show last night. Acknowledging his positive attitude, energy and work ethic, the man offered him a job to go on tour the next morning with the band and also offered him 4 times the amount of money he was currently making. Talk about striking the right chord!

For the next 6 ½ years Craig toured with Air Supply and completely changed the direction of his life. This Lane Change would serve as an opening to travel the road to success that has paved the course of his life ever since. When you shift into a new lane and keep driving forward, it may even merge into a bigger road than you expected.

Performing above and beyond as he always has, Craig was rewarded with an extremely unique opportunity. He went on to work for Guns N' Roses as Axl Rose's personal assistant. Working side by side with a mega personality, Craig soaked up not just their music, but valuable lessons along the way. He understood he was touring with talented bands but what he didn't realize at the time was that he was learning an irreplaceable education on entrepreneurship from some of the most recognizable bands on the planet.

When it comes to any business in any industry, marketing and sales are the key to its success. Rock star bands have an uncanny ability to attract loyal followers who become raving fans and lifelong clients. Craig was learning first-hand how ultra-successful musicians interacted with the media and with their fans, how they filled venues of 80,000 people and what it took to be bigger than life. The experience and instruction Craig received over 10 years touring with legends in the music world helped him obtain the knowledge to teach entrepreneurs how to become rock star marketers when he made a lane change and left the music world to become a full-time entrepreneur.

"We have been marketed to in everything our entire lives. I just feel as an entrepreneur you need to do things different than everybody else. People might not be brazen enough to do the things I do in marketing, even though everyone should. At least our RockStar Marketing strategies get them thinking differently." Craig now hosts extremely successful live boot camps and mentors entrepreneurs, coaches, authors and speakers how to help their businesses rock and roll! Any concept is simply an idea until it is implemented. Then it becomes a tactic. Some of Craig's strategies, when incorporated into your deliberate marketing plan, will completely change your business. For those so bold as to incorporate these into your business, you will go from just another marketer to a RockStar Marketer:

Reverse Shoplifting: Take your book and put it on the shelves in book stores. People work their entire lives to get their books on the shelves of well-known bookstores but you can go place them there yourself today. As an author, what better way to market your business!!

Junk Mail: Take the self-addressed envelope from the junk mail you receive that has paid postage already included. Instead of filling out the survey they are expecting, put a flyer with your promotional material in the return envelope with the statement "Are you stuck in a dead-end job?" They will contact you because you turned propaganda marketed to you in your favor to generate a new lead!

Direct Mail: Send a standard white envelope with nothing inside to your prospects. Include your telephone number under the return address on the outside of the envelope. When they receive it, they will call you because you "forgot" to include what they thought you meant to. Then you acknowledge you didn't intend to send anything and just simply wanted to talk.

Reverse Mastermind: Charge a premium for the first year to exclude those who won't take it seriously. Then honor the members by decreasing the cost each year so that they remain in the community until they get to their goal of staying involved for the most affordable price possible.

Craig has been able to get into the fast lane by shifting his mindset from traditional to radical. It begins with passion. When you do things for the wrong reasons there is nothing you can do right to accelerate your business. You will end up at a dead end wondering how you got there. Yet, when you pursue a road paved with good intentions, driven by desire, you will find the perfect lane for you. If you want to become a rock star, you have to focus and treat your business like a business or it will pay you like a hobby. "The only way an entrepreneur will make it is if they take a risk and just go for it. You have to go all in 100%. Let go of fear or you're never going to make it," Craig suggests.

Living in a place of desperation is a killer. To truly live and thrive you must be confident and become a student of perpetual growth. Your business will increase in direct proportion to your ability to grow personally. Marketing is the ability to get a prospect to know you exist and become interested in what you do. Sales is the ability to empower them into action to close the deal. "If you did one thing in marketing, you would be successful and that's just showing up, physically and mentally."

Mastering the fundamentals in your industry and perfecting your craft, on a never-ending basis, is a key to becoming an expert in your field and getting in to the fast lane. Most people have a destructive mindset and destructive habits, yet expect to construct a 7-figure business. The road to success is always under construction and what we construct in our minds will build the super highway to success or failure.

When you have a solid foundation, you can make the appropriate shifts necessary to drive forward. Even if you need a tune up to increase your skill set along the journey, when you operate your vehicle and fuel it with passion and remain in alignment with your truest desire, your performance will become elite and you can achieve larger than life results. You don't need to reinvent the wheel; just put your own rims on it! For most of us, that means letting go of those things that are holding us back. We put a 'boot' on our own wheels, but expect our lives to move forward smoothly. We build our own speed bumps and then complain that they're in the way.

One night when Craig was touring with Guns N' Roses, Axl and Doug, the manager of GNR who got Craig the job, went to a U2 show. Craig instead partied hard and got completely hammered. And he got nailed for it. Craig missed the limos to get to the planes for the next stop on tour. He was able to get a ride to the airport and as he arrived, the entourage was fortunately still on the tarmac. As he jumped into the limo with Axl and Doug, finding humor and relief in the situation, he got a wake-up call. "I have zero respect for people who drink and get drunk," Doug proclaimed. Delirious partly because he was in a drunken stupor and partly at the astonishment of being admonished for drinking while on tour with Guns N'

Roses, Craig felt as empty as the liquor bottles he had consumed that night.

One year after that defining moment, Craig decided to stop drinking. He hasn't touched alcohol since and attributes much of his success to being straight edged. A drunk mind ultimately speaks a sober heart. When we have an unwavering vision of our lives, we must relinquish our shortcomings in order to go the distance. The tough times transform our capabilities and ultimately a smooth road will not make a skilled driver. The hardships we experience become the catalyst to drive the world forward. The ultimate vice each of us has is the story we have fashioned, which creates the limit on our true potential.

Life is hard but those challenging times allow us to go from SUCKcessful to SUCCESSFUL.We can either have excuses or accomplishments, but not both simultaneously. When you want to get in the fast lane, pick one road that will propel you toward your destination. When we take too many roads we end up nowhere. Like many musicians who become mega rock stars, they are continually innovating. They are proud nonconformists. They do not accept things as they are. The express themselves through innovation and they thrive on creating something to share with the world. Entrepreneurs are much the same. Lane Changers don't believe if it's not broke don't fix it. We believe we need to break the mold, take it apart and rebuild something newer and better. Getting into the fast lane means not walking an old path but paving a new one.

Craig has become a rock star, smashing records and singing all the way to the bank because he is different. He allowed the challenges in his life to become prosperous Lane Changes. Too many entrepreneurs sound like a broken record. Perhaps it's time to march to a different beat. Your message, with the right marketing, can become music to your prospect's ears. It is time to change your tune so you can drum up more business. The world is our stage. It is time to face the music. And your fears. This is your time to get into the fast lane and become a RockStar Lane Changer, bypassing a great life on the way to your greatest life!

# WHEN THE STUDENT IS READY

*"The mediocre teacher tells.*
*The good teacher explains.*
*The superior teacher demonstrates.*
*The great teacher inspires."*
*— William Arthur Ward*

## Daniel Moirao

Teachers play a significant role throughout the course of our lives, and yet often we don't realize their lessons until we truly understand how significantly they impact our lives. Daniel Moirao is the only one of 4 siblings to attend college. Raised by parents who were both high school dropouts, Daniel adopted their hopes for him which were to get a high school diploma, get a good paying job, get married and have kids. That was their view of success.

Throughout school, Daniel was the student that teachers hoped they wouldn't see on their class roster. Classified as a 'problem child,' Danny was known more for his shenanigans than his test scores. To add fuel to the fire, as he was entering 6th grade, his parents divorced. While most of the adolescents in his neighborhood found themselves in jail, Daniel found himself imprisoned by the opinions and judgments of others.Entering junior high, Daniel was assigned to Marsha Weisman, a first-year teacher. While she was his 6th grade teacher, it seemed as though she almost had a sixth sense for what Daniel really needed at that point in his life. And what he would learn that year did not appear in any textbooks. Ms. Weisman challenged Daniel by asking him questions and taking a genuine concern of how he was doing every morning. And while it may seem inconsequential, often the smallest gestures lead to the biggest impressions.

"What is it you want to do in life, Danny?" Settling for what would have been traditional, Daniel had never set high expectations for himself. "Have you ever thought of anything else?" This little encouragement gave Daniel the courage to open to the possibility that he didn't have to let the opinions of others become his reality. When we have someone who challenges us, we often avoid them because they make us get uncomfortable. After graduating from her class, Daniel would constantly drop in to visit her. Daniel was so influenced by Marsha that he sought out her time and attention because she helped him think differently. Our friends and family typically tell us what we want to hear. Our teachers and mentors tell us what we need to hear. "What are your plans for the future," Marsha continued to challenge Daniel. While he had never considered college before, Marsha took him on a tour of UC Berkley. While his family couldn't afford to send him, that campus tour sent him in an entirely new direction.

Daniel went on to attend community college and with no real direction, drifting through school, undecided about what he wanted to study, he needed guidance. Marsha invited him to volunteer in her class during his free time. At lunch, he would eat with his former teachers in the staff lounge. Conversing with the faculty, he gained a new perspective on the teaching profession. Marsha Weisman's acts of illustrating genuine care helped Daniel choose his CAREer. He steadfastly gives a lot of credit to her for helping him get his teaching credentials.

While Daniel didn't ever set out to follow the path he took, the questions she consistently asked him clandestinely paved the path for him. Daniel was a rambunctious student turned into an influential teacher. He eventually went on to become a school principal, discovering that the key principle to leadership is influence. His passion for creating change led him to become a trainer for the California School Leadership Academy. Every position he advanced to in his career afforded him the ability to have more impact on more people. Yet though climbing the ranks within the school system, Daniel still had a desire to teach.

Daniel's heart for the students grew with his own personal growth along his academic journey. More significantly, his passion for helping others who didn't have access to the necessary resources developed. Just as his teachers had done for him, Daniel wanted to help his students and staff realize their full potential. People saw things in Daniel that he didn't see and he was now helping others see in themselves what they didn't realize was there.

Challenged to think bigger by his peers, Daniel realized he was fully capable of becoming a superintendent. He discovered that his network made his work more meaningful and enjoyable. While he had never really set out to achieve such high positions, life rewards us when we lead with our passion. When you set your sights on something and take the necessary steps, you will eventually see them through. While the curriculum would suggest we must follow the guidelines, having an intentional purpose can lead us to achieve things we didn't even realize we set out to accomplish.

As a superintendent, Daniel created super intentions to make a difference. After landing in a school district that was fiscally insolvent and below academic proficiency, Daniel's heart turned to unconditional service.

His passion turned from increasing scores to increasing justice for all. Dominated by low socioeconomic demographics, this school district was unjust and unfair. Daniel's mission became creating equality. He was convicted that DIPLOMACY is greater than a DIPLOMA.

As a student, Daniel had a poor reputation. As a teacher, Daniel had a rich reputation. As a principle, Daniel's reputation preceded him. And as a leader, Daniel gained more than just added influence, he netted the respect from others who had previously never believed in him. When you're appointed to a new position of authority, make it your point to impact the lives of others in a positive way. Throughout our journey, it's important to listen to what's said to us, about us and around us. It's vital that we surround ourselves with people who will challenge us by asking the questions that will help us determine the right answers in our own lives.

Things in life will occupy your time. At the same time, you must focus on what's the next part of your legacy you want to create. Teaching isn't about making really good money, it's about making a really good impact. The riches that come above and beyond the job, come from the influence we can provide.

Daniel's experience as a teacher, principal and superintendent has afforded him the opportunity to start his own consultation firm. His mission and passion of creating his own legacy is based on his ability to help others discover their own. All of our experiences, mentors, accomplishments and setbacks shape our reality. Our lives are neither based on our test scores nor the expectations and opinions of others. It's based on our own introspection and how we use all of our gifts and talents to excel in life. It's a reflection of the actions we take and the lives we touch. On the road of life, we all have lanes we are on. We all have vehicles that take us along the journey.

There is a difference between a map and a set of directions. When you follow a set of directions you will have some achievements. However, ultimately we must all follow a map that allows us the ability to get to our destination based on the opportunities that arise throughout our lives. "If you're on the path you believe you're on, if you're pursuing your passion on the road you're on, you will be taken care of" Daniel believes.

Throughout our academic career we are taught a lesson and then given a test. Throughout the road of life, we are given tests and we must determine the lesson. Even if we are not paid by an educational system, we are all teachers. And we certainly must all remain life-long students, constantly learning. People will put limitations on us. We will put limitations on ourselves. Lane Changers bypass all LIMITations to get into the fast lane.

"You better get right or
you're gonna get left."
~ Geoffrey Bloom

# Dottie Kelley

With an audacious zest for life and a "knowing" sense, Dottie Kelley has traveled the road of life in a way most will never experience. Dottie was 19 when she got married, the first time. Her military man made her laugh and for Dottie, when you make her laugh, you're winning over her heart. He loved her contagious smile. Together, it was always about adventures, drinking and fun. It was a good fit. Dottie always thought she was supposed to get married at a young age, have kids and be a housewife. That's what her parents did, so it just kind of made sense, and she would do the same. There was never much discussion about college or what Dottie "could" be in the future. Often we fall victim to someone else's plan for our life, and what we think we are supposed to do, rather than a life we want to create for ourselves.

So when Military orders came in and the opportunity came up for the couple to be relocated from California to Washington State, it seemed like a great opportunity. This new adventure brought a fresh set of challenges. It gave Dottie and her husband time to be alone. By themselves. Just the two of them. Together, as husband and wife. Immediately, he went to work full-time and started school full-time. The adventure was over. She was lonely in a drizzly place where she felt isolated. No friends, no family, just her husband and a lot of alcohol. Throughout their marriage the only real communication they had was after her husband and her would drink and the "real" communication was constant bickering and fighting.

She decided it was time to find a job and get back to work. But the jobs she found never felt right. Either, they weren't challenging enough or painfully boring. She didn't have the experience or education to start a career and Dottie always wanted that. It was one dead end job after another. There was a constant internal nagging, restlessness. Dottie began to recognize there was so much more for her life and that realization became an opportunity for Dottie to truly discover who she really was. Often times our circumstances and environment force us to become someone, yet Dottie used her circumstances and environment to create who she wanted to become. When we change the way we look at things in life, the things we look at change. When we are looking for new opportunities we often see things in a new way or even see an entirely new opportunity.

Driving around town submitting resumes, Dottie noticed these small coffee shacks on every corner, and they were always busy. Dottie became intrigued and fascinated by this concept she'd never seen before. While she didn't have the money, she had a renewed dream of owning her own business. She researched everything, put lists together and even fantasied what the logo would look like. She was passionate and had a vision. Once that ball got rolling there was no stopping her.

When her husband went to work, Dottie went to work on her dreams. She would sit and imagine the line of cars at her espresso stand and how she would serve them. What would make her business different in an already saturated market? Why would customers go to her espresso stand? What's could she offer that would keep them coming back? What would set her apart from everybody else? This was all Dottie thought about, talked about and dreamed about. Dottie talked to everyone she knew, asking questions and getting feedback about her idea, even from her landlord who was her neighbor. He was also a contractor. He told Dottie he would help her and could built it for a quarter of the price. All she needed now was a location. She went to a local real estate office and asked about locations where she could establish her new business. To her surprise and what seemed like fate, the broker said he had the perfect spot, right in their parking lot! Action creates possibilities. And sometimes we just have to have the beans to take the first steps!

Dottie was very observant about her competition and realized that to be outstanding you have to stand out. She named her business "Polka Dotz" espresso and painted her location hot pink, purple and teal green to attract customers. Her customers would joke about "there being a sale on paint" and it was a great conversation starter. During her research, she learned that coffee was one of the most chemically treated foods in the world. She wanted to offer her customers a healthy coffee option. So she used all organic coffee, made her own homemade whipped creams and offered a non-dairy alternative. Nobody else was doing that. In business, you either need to get right or you're gonna get left.

Get right with your uniqueness, creativity, ambition AND customers. Or you will get left behind! Dottie had this drive her whole life and had found the vehicle to help her to shine. "Once I started visualizing it and imagining myself with my own business, things started to happen. It was unstoppable. I would have never thought a 22-year-old military house wife would have been able to start and run a successful business."

When we have a dream, it's not as much about the resources we have as much as how resourceful we can be! People who don't pursue their dreams usually don't because they see a problem in every situation. Entrepreneurs see a solution in every problem! Moreover, when we move into action and follow our dreams the universe has a funny way of rewarding us, and not always in the ways we anticipate. Dottie created a following of loyal customers and was committed to creating a healthy, memorable experience. She was focused on service and how she could be of service, but there was one significant customer who would actually serve her. He gave her the advice that would completely change the course of her life.

On occasion, and it seemed always at the perfect time, an elderly pastor would come by for his favorite cup of coffee and to visit Dottie. They always had a lot to talk about. She was doing well, and like her beans, her business was in the black. However, she felt like something was missing and she couldn't take her business to the next level. The pastor looked at Dottie and told her "you have to have faith." She didn't know what that meant - she didn't understand the concept of letting go, and how to "just have faith" that everything would work out for the best. Dottie continued to remind herself that faith is not knowing what the future holds, but knowing who holds the future and that there's a grand plan for Dottie.

She continued to build her business, but her focus on growing her company took her away from her health and she found herself overweight and tired. She was always physically athletic and healthy but her health was starting to fade as quickly was her love of the business. Shopping at Target one day, she ran into a friend who she went to junior high school with, back in Lompoc, California. Dottie knew something amazing was going to come out of that chance reunion and felt a calling that they should be doing something together. Her friend just had a baby and was looking to get back in shape, as was Dottie. They both agreed that they wanted to make each other's lives better and committed to regaining their health together. Dottie took this interaction and turned it into another opportunity.

She purchased a pair of in-line skates and started skating around the parking lot to serve her customers. She was able to create more uniqueness, serve more customers, stay active and have fun at the same time! And more importantly, she took this small idea and turned it into one that she could use to change people's lives.

With a growing desire to get back to California, Dottie and her newly rekindled friend decided to in-line skate from Canada to Mexico. They put a plan together and their idea turned into a movement. They called themselves "Pacific Coasters for a Cure." They landed sponsorships from K2 Sports, Clearly Canadian water, Mossimo and Stussy Clothing and they also got a car from Volkswagen so one of Dottie's employees could drive alongside them with all the food and supplies. Because their journey wasn't about the money but rather the cause, they decided to donate the money to muscular dystrophy research as a tribute to her co-founders Aunt who was diagnosed with Lou Gehrig's disease. The day they departed, they agreed "they were on a mission from God." They had faith in their safety and the blessing to be on such a journey. Dressed to the nines in full safety gear, they were off.

The first three days were all about the building, maintaining and constant burning reminder of the blisters brewing on their feet. As they made their way down to Seattle for their official launch party with theirs sponsors, it had mostly been smooth skating. It wasn't until Dottie realized the next day and over 100 miles away, that she had left her backpack filled with the $1500 emergency money, her driver's license and military ID in a restaurant back in Seattle. Luckily enough, she only lived 45 minutes north of Seattle, so getting new IDs only took a day. Of course, she did the right thing and repaid the money she lost. Just a minor set-back.

Often when we start something new it can be a battle getting off to a fast start. When we begin new adventures on the road of life sometimes we hit toll roads and road blocks that for most would send us on a detour that would force us to veer off the road to disaster. Dottie simply put the windshield wipers on her life's challenges and kept driving forward! They arrived at their destination at the boarder gates between Mexico and California only sporting bikinis and bike helmets, bronzed and completely ripped. Unanticipated, the journey ended August 28th, Dottie's 24th birthday.

Dottie felt unstoppable with a newfound confidence and knowing she could now accomplish anything. During her mission she had people counting on her. She never thought about quitting, because she already had the vision of finishing. "There was a start and a finish. It was all about the journey. We had a vision of the finish, and what it looked like and felt like. There was no timeline, we just had to get from point A to point B". It's easy in life to let diversions and detours distract us from accomplishing our goals. Remember, it's all about the journey, keep your foot on the gas, change lanes when you need to and keep moving forward. They key to find your vehicle to greatness is to be open minded and take a different route if you choose. When you live life on purpose and mission, the doors to living life in the fast lane will open. As you drive forward, occasionally you'll need a "designated driver" in life who helps you map out your road to a truly fulfilled life. Every now and then, you just have to remind yourself to "have faith" and get right.

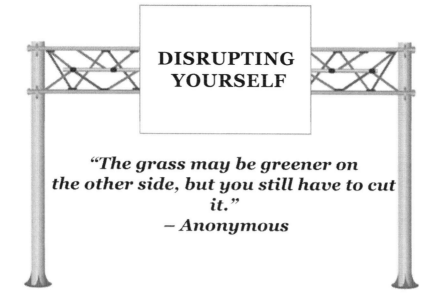

*"The grass may be greener on the other side, but you still have to cut it."*
*– Anonymous*

## Elliot Grossbard

When businesses and individuals go through hard times, they have to challenge how they operate internally and externally. You can say the same thing is true with being in a comfort zone and "great things never came from comfort zones." Elliot Grossbard's first life changing event was when his father passed away when Elliot was 20 years old. The challenging experience of losing his parent and mentor sped up Elliot's outlook on life and he realized that life wasn't a game, nor can it be taken for granted. Despite the circumstances, he realized the wrong outlook and poor attitude is like a flat tire; you can't get very far until you change it.

"If life wasn't a game, I realized that the next step was to see how I can make a difference in the world, and that started with me, my own life" Elliot reflects. Driven as a professional salesperson, like many full-time entrepreneurs, Elliot gave up the 9-5 in exchange for the 24/7 hustle. Yet, because of his commitment to his Jewish religion, there will always be one day with no hustle, the Shabbos. Living the 24/6 lifestyle, leaving one day for

Family, Faith (and Food) is not only for the religious. "With many things in life, you can't knock something if you haven't tried it." Going off the grid for one full day from sunset for 25 hours is something he truly believes is a gift. "Taking off one day with no phone, no internet, no distractions from what is most important to you not only clarifies your mind but refreshes you physically, emotionally, spiritually and energizes you for the week ahead."

Communication, networking, and serving others' needs before his own, fuels his passion for serving his clients and helping people. An entrepreneurial lifestyle involves the constant requirement of reprioritization at any given moment. Entrepreneurs often complain about lack of time, when lack of direction is the real problem. The key to getting into the fast lane is not to prioritize what is on your schedule, but to schedule your priorities. "The more I experience and hear from others that have success, the more I emphasize both for myself and my clients the importance of focusing on the long game, while keep an eye on the short game."

Elliot began his career in sales because it was simply the fastest path to getting a job. He took a position with New Horizons Computer Learning Center in the 90's when Microsoft's Windows 95 first launched. When he decided to put the same hours in the day contacting companies instead of individuals, Elliot landed a contract with a publicly traded company and broke the company record for the first quarter sales. "More than the commission, more than the high from the sale...the realization that I was able to help someone, and build a relationship that had an impact on their business or life, meant the world to me," Elliot recalls. One of his favorite quotes that hangs in his office is "Stop Selling and Start Helping" by Zig Ziglar. So he stopped selling to others and started to help.

The lessons Elliot learned at his first sales experience began his foundation for how he would sell; he would help others. His way of building relationships in his genuine way, attracted other opportunities. He was approached by a member of his community who was managing approximately $500 million in assets. This executive was seeking a junior partner because he was looking to create a work-life balance. His values closely aligned with Elliot's vision for his life and he gladly accepted the opportunity. Even though he wasn't building his own book of business, which would have afforded him a better income, the education and experience he gained was priceless.

Self-awareness is a topic of one of his mentors and friends, Gary Vaynerchuck, a successful businessman and social media expert that Elliot credits most of his skills and knowledge of social media to. "When Gary started making a great effort to get people to be real with themselves, I looked back to try to relate and internalize it." Reminiscing about growing up he recalls excelling at two things in particular, basketball and singing. "I used to tape each game Michael Jordan played on WGN, the Chicago cable channel #33 as it came free on our TV set. I use to try to emulate Air Jordan from the way he shot his free throws (dribbled the ball two times followed by a backwards ball flip) to his jump shot. (Left hand flicked to the left as the shot went off.)"

One of Jordan's go-to moves and therefore Elliot's was, when driving to the basket, rising to the hoop for a layup and then swooping from one side of the basket to the other side for a reverse layup while keeping great hang time. "It was just one of those things I mastered, it looked cool too, but I hated to look at anyone running down the court because the one thing I have always despised, "the showoff", was the one thing I never wanted to be associated with. It was a struggle for me, I had talent and enjoyed the game immensely but I hated the spotlight."

With a separate but equal passion for music, he remembers a time during the high holidays as a kid, sitting next to his father, singing harmony with the cantor leading the services. Suddenly a family friend sitting nearby shouted "Grossbard get up there!". Getting an approval and nudge from his father, he went up to the middle of the Synagogue in front of the entire congregation and started singing along. Even though he was embarrassed, he got lost in the moment. It was another "lane changing" moment for Elliot as he fell in love with the idea of leading his own services one day, and has been for the last 23 years (Jordan's jersey number is just a coincidence) in places like Florida, Virginia and Georgia.

Both of those recollections have in common the importance of being self-aware of the things that you are strong in. as well as your weaknesses. "Thankfully I got over the uncomfortable feeling of being in the spotlight and embraced the gifts I was given."

"Take a moment, right now and get real with yourself. Think about what you are really good at, what others ask help from you with, and what you enjoy doing professionally. The high majority of those that will be reading this will notice they are pretty much the same thing. What you are good at is what you enjoy doing and vice versa. Now think about what you are and what you are not great at."

**My Strengths:** Networking, Sales, Marketing, Connecting with People.

**My Weaknesses:** Paperwork, Organizing my desk, my office, office work.

Go ahead and write yours down. Yes, right now.

Strengths:

_____

_____

Weaknesses:

_____

_____

Now tweet a pic of it to @ElliotOneT

 "Realize that what you just wrote down will often be a lane changing event. If you are one of the lucky ones who is currently making a living doing what they enjoy naturally to do, then you are truly blessed and as my oldest mentor Harvey Mackay says,"

"Find something you love to do and you'll never work a day in your life"

 Speaking of luck, people often consider luck that plays a part of success and asking Elliot about it, he brings to light a "different" way to look at luck. "Mazel Tov!" are words you most certainly have heard before. Literally translated as "Good Luck", it is used to express congratulations for a significant occasion or accomplishment. "The word Mazel (Luck) is made up of 3 Hebrew letters with each representing respectively – place, time and speech. You can then say we create our own luck by being in the right place, at the right time, and saying the right thing. My big brother (by choice) David argues with me on this and says it actually stands for being in the right place, at the right time, and having put in the time to learn and prepare for that situation. Either way, in a sense you really do create your own luck. (Thank You David.)"

Elliot has learned important lessons in his career and has gathers core values that continue to build on the foundation of how he conducts himself in life and business:

- Realizing the customer IS your business is essential; without the customer there IS no business.
- Treat everyone like a human being. Say please and thank you. Smile and talk to people they aren't robots, yet.
- Put yourself in your customer's shoes regularly. You can't understand your customer if you have not been one yourself.
- You are going to make mistakes and that's okay, but only if you use them to learn from.
- Be different, think different, act different. Today just being a gentlemen and *Mensch\**, will make you stand out. (*a respectful and caring person)

In life, we have two choices: become an entrepreneur or work for one.

Elliot was ready for a Lane Change.

Growing as a salesperson, Elliot discovered he wanted to start his own business. Moreover, he wanted to start a business that operated on these and other core values and principles. In building a book of business on your own and from scratch you need to look at who you are targeting. When you want to increase your ROI, increase your contact with POIs. Persons of Influence or Interest are the keys to growing your business. The challenge is to identify who exactly the right POI is you should target.

After successfully running his own company for a few years, Elliot launched Disruptive Sales, a Sales and Marketing consulting company. Disruptive Sales works with existing companies, brands, or startups and individuals who have stagnant sales, dull or confusing brands, ineffective marketing, helping them grow by disrupting their current tactics, and improving company culture and morale.

Elliot approaches a full-spectrum approach from the sales force to top management. He essentially becomes a member of their company by going on sales calls with the sales staff, sits in company strategy sessions; in short he makes his client's company his company. Through his process, together with his client they create innovative ways to market their products and services, often leading to new streams of revenue from never-before-thought-of-clientele and markets. His startup ZeeKah which means "rapport" in Hebrew, helps salespeople and companies build rapport and gain relationships at a much quicker pace cutting the sales cycle by 1/3.

The traditional sales process is archaic:

1) Introduction
2) Schedule a meeting or call
3) Discovery about the company, product or prospect
4) Follow up to the meeting / Call
5) Establish rapport
6) Build and earn trust
7) (Hopefully) Close the deal

One of the things Elliot openly doesn't agree with Gary Vaynerchuk previously mentioned, who publicly says he does not read books is to do just the opposite. One of the keys of business is consistently trying to get better at what you are doing. Always be learning, sharpening your tools, and one of the best ways to do that is reading books from experts in your field, or other industries that you have interest in.

"I was not always an avid reader, in fact growing up the only things I consistently read were the daily sports page and the Sunday comics." That all changed when Elliot was in his mother's husband's office in upstate New York. "I saw on his bookshelf this little red book that caught my eye titled just that, The Little Red Book of Selling by Jeffery Gitomer. That was literally a life changing moment for me," Elliot says. Picking up his own copy at the airport on the way home, he was blown away at the content he was reading, all surrounding the place where he spent practically every day, sales.

"I immediately started consuming content on sales and marketing. Up until then everything I was doing in my sales career just felt natural. Now after reading the likes of Dale Carnegie, John Maxwell and Harvey Mackay, I was being opened up to new ideas and strategies of how to help people." Since then he has accumulated many favorite authors and continues to do so as he sets out to read 3-5 books a month. Reading is really a good way to get yourself out of a funk and gets your mind thinking of new ideas and practices and adventures.

Elliot wraps it up with "If I had to leave you with something to take away, some of it would be":

- **Find your passion and feed it**. You might not be able to do this at different times in your life, (ex. finances, family responsibilities), but there is always time for a side hustle now, for when that time comes.
- Love what you do and help others do the same.
- Grab a book, put on some music and get away.
- You are not alone, collaborate! It really is like magic when like-minded people get together.
- You **are** different, might as well act that way!

- Know WHO you are, WHY you are doing it, WHAT you are driving towards, and the HOW will appear to you.
- If you want to accomplish something, you have to work hard, really hard.
- If you don't go for something and don't ask for it, you'll never know if the answer is yes or no.
- And finally from my father, "If you are going to do something, do it right the first time or better to not do it at all."

# Frank Shankwitz

There are people you meet throughout life who win your heart instantly because they possess the genuine desire to help others. Frank Shankwitz is a man that has changed the world and has literally changed the lives of millions of people. Frank has altered giving as we know it by granting wishes for people around the world. He is a man that founded one of the most recognizable non-profits which has funded over a billion dollars for people who never imagined how their lives would be impacted because of his heart. Moreover, he has not taken any profit for himself because his payback is seeing the smiles on the faces of the recipients and the difference that it has made in their lives through the Make-A-Wish Foundation.

The beautiful thing about life is that to make a huge difference and change everything for someone, it doesn't always have to cost anything. Frank was raised very poor by his vagabond mother. Throughout his childhood people took care of them, fed and clothed them. Frank was forced to get a job as a dishwasher at 10 years old. Early on, he discovered how to fend for himself but he also learned he was able to get by because of the constant help and support from others.

Every person we interact with has an influence on us and symbiotically we have an influence on them. One of the most influential people in Frank's life was Juan, who had become somewhat of a father figure in Frank's life. Juan had a paramount impact on his life. Most significantly Juan told him one day "Frank when you can someday, give back." Frank's initial reaction was one of scarcity, responding, "What do you mean? We can't even take care of ourselves." Frank learned about giving back with the abilities and assets he had, not necessarily the resources he thought he needed.

Frank determined early on and throughout high school that he wanted to fill up his cup first, meaning he wanted to become someone that would be able to selflessly give because of the person he would become. Like many, money drove Frank's direction and he went to work as a technical engineer at Motorola which allowed him to become more financially secure. However, Frank didn't want a safe, secure life. He wanted a life marked by adventure and significance. He was an adrenaline junkie and Frank gave up a well-positioned, high end job as an engineer to become an Arizona Highway Patrol as a motorcycle officer with their early motorcycle program.

Most officers believe in a higher power and every time he started his shift Frank would say, "Please allow me to come home today" and when he would get home he would graciously say "thank you for allowing me to come home." While serving the force, during a high speed chase, Frank was in a life-changing accident and was pronounced dead on the scene. But God had different plans and wanted to use Frank to change the world.

During his recovery Frank questioned his purpose and every day ask himself and God, "Why did I survive this?" Because of that accident Frank discovered his lane change – his mission and purpose in life. Throughout life we are put in positions that lead us down the roads that open up the opportunity for us to discover our true purpose and how we can impact lives during our mission. In 1980 Frank was introduced to Christopher, a 7-year-old boy with Leukemia who only had a couple weeks to live. His dream - his wish - was to become a highway patrol motorcycle officer like his heroes Ponch and John from the television show Chips. Through the effort of their police department, his doctor and his mother, Frank got to meet Chris. Frank's heart broke for Chris and Frank wanted to help make Chris' dream a reality.

Through Frank's effort, Chris got to sit on a motorcycle and they helped him become the first and only honorary highway patrol officer in the history of the Arizona Highway Patrol. He was outfitted with a custom uniform, officer badge, Smokey hat and motorcycle wings – everything that made him not just believe his was an officer but allowed him to become an official officer like his heroes. He passed away a couple days later and Frank believes that his motorcycle wings helped carry him to heaven that day. Frank discovered that Chris was going to be buried in a little town in Southern Illinois and Frank insisted that they give Chris a full police burial.

On the flight home from the funeral, Frank began thinking "here's a boy who had a wish and we made it happen. Why can't we do that for other children? Let them make a wish and we will make it happen." Make-A-Wish was born from the simple act of helping someone else make their dream come to life when he was merely fighting for his own life. Within 6 months the organization was up and running and by November 1980 they were official and in 1981 they granted their first wish. "Someday we will be granting wishes all over the world" Frank stated and his board members laughed at him. But the key in life is too laugh in the face of adversity and don't take the opinions of others personally. Frank turns the negatives into positives and while he does not always know how he keeps driving forward.

The Make-A-Wish Foundation currently has 63 chapters in the United States and 36 international chapters. They have granted 350,000 wishes and somewhere in the world a wish is granted every 26 minutes. To create success, people believe they need to do whatever it takes in their own life to get ahead. In reality, being of contribution and helping others get what they want allows people to create true success. Take care of your mission and the world will take care of you. And it starts with a choice.

Frank couldn't be a police officer and run Make-A-Wish. Frank loved being an officer and didn't have the knowledge he needed to run a non-profit. He surrounded himself with experts, people in the non-profit world, who had experience. Frank quickly learned to seek the experts, seek their counsel and hire them. Recently retired after 41 years as a police officer, Frank's legacy as an officer still makes a difference in the force. And the force had an impact in his life as he moved on.

Being a police officer taught him to read people, understand them and appreciate that everyone has a story. He also discovered how to discern truth from fiction in people's lives. He learned to be assertive and always rely on your values. He was told over and over "you can't do that" and he learned how to turn the negative to the positive. As Frank was living "Life in the Fast Lane" as a highway police officer he always remembered to have fun throughout his 41 years of service.

He was eventually promoted to detective in narcotics and because of his knowledge of engineering and ability to reconstruct accidents they assigned him to homicide where he truly found his passion. Often we question why we do what we do until it benefits us later in life. When leaders see something in you, they want to channel that expertise so you need to trust them. Follow their advice and it will lead to unbelievable opportunities. During life's challenges and life or death situations it's paramount to trust in yourself, trust in your instincts and trust in your training. Throughout life we have our own 'life or death' situations such as divorce, bankruptcy or the death of a loved one. These adversities challenge us tremendously. But from a challenge we can create a lane change. These life changing lane changes define the direction our life goes.

After his biggest lane change, Frank continued to make a difference. As an adrenaline junkie at his advanced senior years, he's been given the opportunity to get involved in movie making and television production. Through his connections and the people he's helped through the Make-A-Wish Foundation, doors have opened and Frank's wishes are coming true. Surrounding himself and his people with the experts so they can make it happen. Today, he encourages others to find something where you want to go to work every day and you want to stay there and enjoy it. When you do what you love you have the ability to fill your own cup first.

Frank believes that "Character is developed, not inherited." You have to rely on your mentors, your own motivational standards and your own moral standards. It wasn't about success for myself, it was for others. "I want to give back because so many people have given to me." With hundreds of thousands of wishes granted around the world, Frank's wish is to be able to financially help his family who is scattered around the country.

Both of Frank's daughters are doing motorcycle rides to help wounded warriors. That generational cycle of giving back is ongoing. Their family legacy is the most important component in the journey for Frank. If you want to get in the fast lane, find a purpose. To do that, follow your dreams.

Make a wish; the best way to make that wish come true is to help someone else make their dreams come true first.

> My wish for you
> Is that this life becomes all that you want it to
> Your dreams stay big, your worries stay small
> You never need to carry more than you can hold
> And while you're out there gettin' where you're gettin' to
> I hope you know somebody loves you
> And wants the same things too
>
> I hope you never look back but you never forget
> All the ones who love you
> And the place you left
> I hope you always forgive and you never regret
> And you help somebody every chance you get
> Oh, you find God's grace in every mistake
> And always give more than you take

-Rascal Flatts

# Gina Ruby Puterbaugh

Gina Ruby Puterbaugh glimmers with passion while a joyful smile permanently radiates on her face creating an almost inexplicable aura of positivity and an unequivocal zest for life. Her foundation moralities of life began in her youth as she discovered that what is in your soul as a child is the key. When Gina was 9 years old her parents transitioned from the corporate world to entrepreneurship and her family went from the big city to a dude ranch in the Rockies. She had gone from city to country and while she it was nurture that created her childhood it was nature that now surrounded her. Gina was the baby of the family. Seeds were planted that eventually turned into fruitful opportunities. Those seeds became her lane changes.

What she would eventually discover during the transition was that her parents had lost it all during that changeover. She learned early on that it is acceptable to take risks and to lose everything because you can always build back up. She became comfortable with the concept of reinventing yourself and thanks to her parents, entrepreneurship comes naturally to Gina. Gina got dialed into entrepreneurship during her childhood. That's also where her faith was built because her parents were full of integrity and their love for the Lord was refreshing. Risk taking and faith were foundational. And she grasped that God loved her so she loved him back. It just made sense to her.

Gina admits that her mom and dad were her greatest mentors and still continue to be influential in her empire-building journey. They are Gina's heroes. One of the predominating themes in her life that permeates her everyday living is that she does the right things for her. Those things that society would deem "normal" such as drinking, drugs and sex were not what appealed to her. What drove Gina was the desire to help others and live abundantly and healthy.

As Gina was growing up in her new environment after the move, she had a friend who was overweight. It was sad for her to see her friend getting picked on and emotionally bullied. Because of her heart for others and her desire to help those she cared about, Gina made a commitment that she wanted to support people to fully love life and completely love themselves.

Gina attended a Christian college and her passion for health and wellness grew yet she didn't want to go down the traditional route of being a doctor or nurse. She got degree in education, music and Biblical studies. Two weeks after graduation she moved to San Diego because in the 4th grade she did a report on the city and realized there was never any snow!

She instantly fell in love and when she arrived she worked at a Christian college and traveled and did music. Two years after moving to SD she married a pastoral student. She stared acting and modeling while also acting as a youth minister. She thought this was going to be her life for the rest of her life. However, as we all know speed bumps and roadblocks on the road of life can create lane changes and send us in a new direction. As Gina was approaching 40 and they had been married for 13 years, her husband "found greener pastures." Gina went through a divorce and had to learn that lesson that even if you do everything right it doesn't guarantee you a bed of roses.

She became sad and depressed for a month, sleeping nearly 18 hours a day. During that season she wasn't making any money and she realized she needed to start creating her life. Many of the times we think that the grass is greener on the other side and we fail to realize that it's often fertilized with manure. The reality is that the grass is greener where we water it. She made a conscious decision to brush it off and take the next step forward. She discovered that God brings people in your life when you need them the most. She was exposed to personal development and she met a mentor who coached people that made 6 figures or more. She began to create a shift around her money mindset and her big picture vision. This shift led to creating massive success in her life the way she wanted her life to turn out.

Every other month Gina invested in a personal development course. She was a sponge for mentoring. God was her anchor and others were her coaches. She understood that healing takes time and it takes time to get the healing. Because of the challenges that came with her she wanted to be healed as quickly as possible and she did the work to heal and grow. You cannot help if you've been victimized; you can however choose to go from victim to victor. She was Chosen for the Kingdom and she believes because of that she has a choice.

Often when we make a lane change we want to see the results immediately. We can make quick decisions but sometimes we experience delayed gratification. Gina still had no money and no assets. Yet because the windshield is bigger than the rearview mirror she was looking back only long enough to learn from the past but looking ahead to create her future. She resonated with a verse in Isiah that claims she would be bestowed upon her a "crown of beauty instead of ashes, the oil of joy instead of mourning, and a garment of praise instead of a spirit of despair." She had an unwavering faith and confidence that He can take the biggest messes and make it into a beautiful masterpiece.

She decided to retire from modeling and contribute to society in a profound way. Her passion for health and wellness fueled that passion. She was introduced to a network marketing opportunity with a reputable company. She wanted to be her own boss and didn't want to reinvent the wheel so she went to work and ultimately found her true passion. Most never step into and drive that vehicle. Gina got into the Fast Lane. When she started following her passion and took care of herself, doors started opening. She instills in others that when you love yourself and have the foundation of faith, the desires of your heart will show up. God's timing is everything and she was ready to receive opportunities!!

Gina had the road map of who she wanted in her life and who she didn't. She allowed God to be in the driver seat, especially when it came to her relationships. Because of her disappointing previous relationship she created a list of 29 "non-negotiables" that were paramount to date someone. When she was introduced to her future husband she simply wanted to be friends but nothing more. His love of the Lord created a challenge because she thought she would be single for the rest of her life. She began falling for the man who she thought was too good to be true. Her husband Andy is attractive man not just because of his physical looks but because he is confident in who he is as a man. He is selflessly capable of loving Gina for who she is as a confident woman. He appreciates her and wants her to be the best version of herself rather than feel overshadowed by who he is and what he's accomplished. He is very patient, understanding and supportive of her active lifestyle. He's a rock in her life and together they lean on their eternal Rock. Their faith is the foundation for their fellowship and stewardship of their gifts.

Gina was happily married to Andy yet there was still a void in her life but because she had always wanted to have a baby but due to infertility, she was incapable of having her own child. However, by God's mercy and grace, through marrying Andy, she was blessed with a step-daughter and she couldn't have asked for a better maternal relationship. Because of her love for Andy and his daughter, Gina replaced what she couldn't have with what was gifted to her. The dreams she had as a child have been surpassed. Gina's blessings continued to flood in as she took her business to six-figures in the first 2 years. With her newfound success, however, she started to revert back to negative thought patterns that created a proverbial glass ceiling for her. She had to commit herself back to focusing on personal development. She discovered that the more she made the more she could bless others.

Her goals are focused on being able to help three times the number of people through increasing her income. She believes that the more she makes the more she can graciously and unconditionally give and that ultimate blessing would be the frosting on top of the cake (with no extra sugar of course). To whom much is given, much will be required and to whom much is entrusted, they will demand that much more. And she loves and thrives on that responsibility. Gina is constantly reminded that it's easy to be happy when things are going well but that's external. Joy comes from the soul. Even when things are chaotic, there is always something to be joyful about. But sometimes you really have to dig to find that joy. There is a big difference between being able to enjoy life and being IN JOY.

Joy is a choice. Gina challenges her friends and clients to focus on what's going well with a foundation of gratitude and thankfulness. She recognizes that in order to get a grip on life you have to get a grip on the steering wheel that will drive the world forward in the direction you want it to go. Gina's love for life comes from the joy she gets by helping others reach their goals and dreams. She knows that everyone has the ability to make a difference in the world and that as long as you're still on this world you have a purpose. And it starts with finding the beauty and the joy in today. The past is over. The future is unknown. But you can always live in the moment.

Treat each other with respect simply because it's the right things to do and moreover you don't know what they're going through. When you fall down, get back up and stop wallowing in your pity. Let it go. You have to make a choice to release it and replace it with something better. That will allow you to get to the place you love. Sometimes you have go through the pain and follow the process and make mistakes to help you grow. When you're stuck or discontent, surround yourself with people who will inspire you, encourage you and motivate you. Follow the leaders because they help you make less mistakes. Yet it's your responsibly to take massive action. Recognize people for who they are and what they have to offer and validate people's integrity. Life is a choice. What are you going to choose today to "Awaken your worth," "Live your God-given purpose" and "Make a difference in the world?"

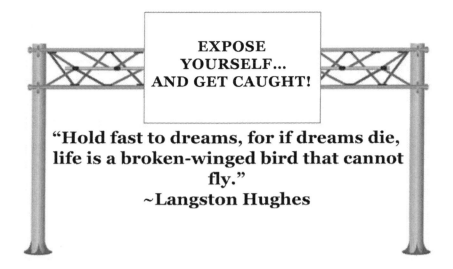

"Hold fast to dreams, for if dreams die, life is a broken-winged bird that cannot fly."
~Langston Hughes

# Greg Writer

Throughout life we get pulled in different directions and we are either pushed by our fears or pulled by our dreams. Some of us are born into a family that determines our direction and some of us need to give birth to the desire to change lanes. Greg Writer was forced early on to determine who he was going to get his values and information from. He was born into a wealthy family but his parents divorced when he was 2. He lived with his mother who had a pattern of getting married and divorced many times. However, while she was entrepreneurial and struggled financially, she always taught him that he was able to have anything and be anything he wanted. In the summers Greg would visit his father, who was extremely wealthy and very generous. Yet in Greg's eyes, his father didn't necessarily possess anything radically special that separated him from anyone.

His father lived next door to the owner of the Denver Broncos and lived fairly extravagantly. Greg would often hop his father's fence and hang out with the NFL athletes. He got a taste of wealth and enjoyed the flavor and determined that was the lifestyle he wanted. Greg made a decision that he wanted to be on the wealthy side of the fence. And in life it takes an unwavering commitment to know what you want, what you don't want and determine what you're willing to pay to get the life you want. The only thing you get by sitting on the indecision fence is splinters in your butt.

When we determine the road of success we want to travel, the right lane will open up. The world conspires for us and opportunities appear as long as we are willing to recognize them as such. Too often as we drive through life and bugs splat on our windshield, our focus turns to those distractions rather than the rest of the clear windshield. In life, we do the same thing, yet those bug splats appear as divorce, health issues, financial struggles, personal insecurities, unhealthy relationships and other circumstantial challenges. We must remain focused on the clear picture of our future rather than the distractions that get in our way.

When Greg determined he wanted success, his oldest brother gifted him the book "Think and Grow Rich." Adopting the philosophy and the principles in the book, Greg realized when it comes to being an entrepreneur, the two biggest factors to increase the chance for massive success were commitment and discipline. The two earliest activities that helped Greg practice commitment and discipline were falconry and hang gliding. He began learning and practicing, mastering his craft. In order to train the majestic birds to fly to you and hunt for you, your discipline needs to be sky high. The survival of the birds was dependent on Greg's ability to master his skills, and in order to master his skills he needed ardent commitment and enthusiastic discipline.

He began getting a bird's eye view of accomplishment and realized that when you combine commitment with consistent discipline, you can literally sore to new heights. And the skills he learned from his hobby were transferred into entrepreneurship. "If you have that kind of discipline of doing the same thing over and over and over for long periods of time, you're guaranteed to have success."

And Greg did just that. The first business Greg founded became a prosperous real estate advertising magazine. His entrepreneurial spirit went into full drive. One day visiting his father, he noticed some stock confirmations and became intrigued. Greg began asking questions and after his dad disclosed he made nearly 6 million dollars profit for the year (this was in 1980), Greg made his first career lane change. His dad started to educate him about investing and even helped him make his first investment, turning $2,000 into $14,000 in 4 months. But the only way he was able to do this was because his dad had invested $100,000 in the same deal. While his dad made $700,000 in 4 months through the same deal, Greg realized it wasn't the money that was important, but rather the exposure to the opportunity that was the true value. Greg quickly understood that when you're around the right people you'll have a higher probability of financial success. Greg believes that the rich really do get richer because of the exclusive exposure that not everyone is fortunate enough to be privy to.

Greg leveraged his family name and went all in. He got his securities license and at age 21 he became the youngest owner of a full-service investment banking firm in the country. Greg learned early that our environment and the people we surround ourselves with shape the decisions and lifestyle we create. Making $20,000 a month on Wall Street makes you susceptible to what money can buy. We all have opportunities and challenges that we get exposed to which shape our future. Greg followed his nose to get into the industry and eventually, for years, most of the money he made ended up going up his nose.

He became addicted to cocaine and the demons that came with it. Again, Greg had to decide which side of the fence he wanted to be on. He got clean and hasn't touched any substances in 28 years. His family and his wife became more important to him and saved his life. He rediscovered his faith and as a born-again Christian, his life was truly saved. Finding a new purpose, he retired from that phase of his life and moved on, in order to move up. Often in life we wait until the time is right to get started. The best time to get started is always now. Ready. Fire. Aim. Until you find the right target for you. Then you must aim and fire when you've got everything ready.

Greg and his team were responsible for raising the initial $600,000 for the Home Shopping Network. Despite cable television being brand new and nothing having ever been sold on television before, Greg believed in the individual and his vision. Through investing into businesses, Greg created 'Torrential Downpour Economics,' the ability to create a flood of new jobs and new products because of the new market that was opened. Raising money for a start-up company, he was able to hand a check for $5 million to an entrepreneur. As tears of gratitude leaked down his face, Greg fell in love with supporting and coaching entrepreneurs.

He had fallen in love with helping make someone's vision become a reality, thus changing the future for so many others as a result. "I think from an entrepreneurial standpoint, you need to surround yourself with people that will support you. You need to get the wisdom and the knowledge from other people who can get you there and accomplish things without going through the pain and the mistakes that they did." As a true entrepreneur and investor, you must be strategic. When it comes to raising capital, much like in most things in life, there is a sequence that will give you the highest probability of acquiring the desired outcome. You must determine who you want to mentor you, who you want to partner with, who you want to joint venture with and then you must give and serve first. Today, you can be a copycat marketer and follow those who have the information, wisdom and tactics to help you get where you want.

And then you must become relentless in your pursuit. Top level people value persistence. In the beginning it may appear to be annoying but if you do it professionally it will turn into respect because of your tenacity. People respect others who know what they want, consistently go after it and never give up. You need to become strategically selfless. And you simply need to understand the success formula in order to obtain your desired outcome:

- Understand the Sequence
- Methodically, strategically and tactically figure out what you need
- Look better, perform better, present better
- Execute effectively
- Market, market, market, market, market, market and then market some more

Greg suggests that the thousands of people who approach him for money don't actually need money; they need coaching and mentoring. When it comes to getting into the fast lane and accelerating the odometer to take it into overdrive, "Most entrepreneurs don't move the needle as fast as they want to because they don't have clarity and because they don't have clarity they aren't focused. You must get clarity on every aspect of your business. Once you get clarity, it's easy to stay focused, but you must have a commitment to yourself, to your plan, and to your vision."

Once you commit to your vision, success will chase you. Products don't create wealth. Systems don't create wealth. People create wealth.

When it comes to getting what want, often it's not always what you think you need. The easy road is always under construction so plan an alternate route and stay in your lane! The grass is not always greener on the other side of the fence. The grass is greener where you water and fertilize it with resolute commitment and fundamental discipline.

"There is only one thing that is impossible:
That's to beat a man who doesn't give up"
— Conor McGregor

# Haris Reis

There are moments in our life that often seem so faint but can speak so loudly to us if we actually listen and respond. Haris Reis has created success from those, realizing that every positive thought and every positive reaction propels you in the right direction. As a member of DECA in high school, Haris began his journey pursuing what he loved by being attentive to everything, even despite the perceived significance of certain things. When he first heard Laymon Hicks, one of the nation's top youth speakers, Haris like many others, was inspired. Yet, like many who are inspired in life, Haris didn't think much about it or do much about it either.

He went off to college and had forgotten about that event. Later, however, he would look back to realize how dramatically it had changed his life and the course of his new life. He realized that other people's messages could change the way he viewed life and if he changed his actions, he would create different results.

Haris was in college and got an email about an organization named CEO. It was made for aspiring entrepreneurs in college. He saw that they were going to Chicago and they were going to be around other college entrepreneurs and some extremely successful business owners, such as the founder of MapQuest and Barefoot wine. Haris listened to a whisper that told him he had to go and he sent an email to the president; thankfully, she responded immediately because the event was in two days. Haris did not know anyone in the organization but knew he had to be at the event. He immediately bought his tickets and was off to Chicago. Little did Haris know that this trip was going to change his life forever!

After being influenced by Bert Gervais' presentation, Haris had the unique opportunity to approach him and talk. He mentioned that he had heard Laymon speak the year prior and as life would have it, Bert happened to be friends with Laymon. As Haris would discover along his journey into the world of personal development, speakers want to support those who are willing to do what it takes to create success. Bert introduced Haris to Laymon and that set him on a quest to learn how he, too, could be on stage.

We have all had that tug on our hearts to pursue our dreams. Haris quickly realized that if he wanted to get where he wanted to go he had to surround himself with the people who would support him along the way. He also needed to pay attention to the doors that were being opened and even if they were just cracked, he had to knock and open them no matter what. As Haris continued his college career, he kept hearing "whispers," quiet nudges of opportunity. Often we are expecting a cataclysmic sign to give us the answers to our questions in life. Yet, the reality is the often it's the subtlest hints that leave clues to guide us along our path.

Receiving an unexpected email about an event, Haris realized that this could be his Kairos moment. The event was going to feature one of his role models – Kevin Harrington, one of the original investors on Shark Tank. This event was 8 months away but Haris heard a whisper that he needed to be around Kevin before this event. Haris had a vision that he would moderate for Kevin and break history because no other college student has moderated someone into the Hall of Fame. It was a mountain of a goal but Haris was determined and he visualized it every day.

As Haris was sitting in class, he would research events Kevin would be speaking at and noticed the Shark-Made Millionaire's tour! Haris heard the whisper and it told him that was the event he would meet Kevin. In between classes, with only 15 minutes to accomplish what he needed, Haris bought a plane ticket to San Diego and rented a hotel. He knew at that moment, from that point forward, when he had an opportunity that he knew would propel him in the direction of his dreams, he was going to seize it, regardless of his circumstances and limited resources.

Soon, he discovered that some of the people we are closest to can feel the most distant when we pursue our dreams. When he asked his mom for a ride to the airport she laughed, inquiring about what he was thinking and why he would possibly go from Nebraska to San Diego to meet a man he didn't even know. What she didn't see yet, was his vision.

Without vision, man perishes. But Haris had a vision that was making him feel more alive than ever! And those around him started to feel his energy and support him. Excited, as he arrived in San Diego he got more and more enthusiastic. He was getting closer to meeting the one person he knew would change his life. He was also excited to meet Loral Langemeier, 5-time New York bestselling author, speaker, wealth coach, and is known as the millionaire maker. What he didn't realize was that sometimes the people we meet are the ones who can open doors for us along the way that we wouldn't be able to open on our own. The power of association was about to become very real for Haris.

While the event didn't start until 9AM the next morning, Haris was so excited that he got to the event at 5AM. He wanted to be the first person inside, recognizing that leaders sit in the front. As the doors opened and he made his way in, expecting to be surrounded by so many other aspiring entrepreneurs, he realized there were only 6 other people were in attendance, including the speakers. Most people want to learn from the experts but most don't take the steps to actually move forward. Haris did, step by step and that's all that mattered. Yet, despite taking the right steps, Kevin Harrington, the man he traveled halfway across the country to meet, didn't even show up.

Haris realized at that moment that sometimes unmet expectations can still turn into blessings as long as you don't give up. Loral was there to speak and Haris purchased her program, despite not having the funds available. You don't always have to have the resources as long as you are resourceful.

When he arrived home, disappointed but refreshed, knowing that his journey wasn't over, he got a message from Loral's company. Because of his desire to succeed and his courage to say YES  and figure out how, they ended up scholarshipping him for the event. Another "whisper" This event was attended by over 300 people, one of whom happened to be Kevin Harrington's uncle.  Kevin's uncle had heard from Loral that Haris was a go getter. As they conversed, Kevin's uncle prepped Haris how to maximize his time with Kevin as he would only have one minute since everyone wanted to connect with him. Haris went to his hotel that night and since there was no TV and the doors would not lock, he stayed up the entire night practicing his pitch.

As he was continuing to practice, refine and rehearse his message that he was going to deliver to Kevin. Consistency is the key to success and Haris was there at 5 am again. Haris saw Kevin in the hallway and he was surrounded by people. This was his chance! Haris, confident as possible, went out and approached Kevin. What would come out of Haris' mouth was nothing like he had practiced. Mumbling some incoherent message, Haris had experienced what others may deem as failure. But in reality he had still made an impression with the man he wanted to impress. And sometimes it's not necessary to be impressive to make an impression. He made an effort when most would have stayed in their comfort zone. And leaders honor action, not perfection.

The next morning, Kevin's uncle saw Haris and approached him. Haris proceeded to share that he met Kevin outside in the lobby the night before and that his approach was miserable. Kevin's uncle acknowledged him for doing what others may not have attempted and reassured him that he would have another chance. Later that day, Haris saw Kevin and approached him. Naturally, he struck up a conversation but this time it was different. Haris hadn't practiced anything. Naturally, he was himself and the outcome was so much better. Little did Haris know that the crowd of 300 kept telling Kevin about him and Kevin was excited to have a regular conversation with Haris.

He realized that day that he should just approach people as people. We are all the same, we just have different experiences and different accomplishments. But when you treat people not as you wish to be treated but as they wish to be treated, doors open up. Another whisper. Because of Haris' confidence, belief and willingness to make moves, people took notice. The 'gurus' started acknowledging him for who he was and what he was going to become and they began to introduce Haris to other leaders because of his initiative.

He now had the itch; he had become an official "seminar junkie" and fell in love with connecting and powering up, associating with people who were at a higher level than him. This was a new chapter in his journey and ironically at his next event he decided he wanted to write a book. Loral connected him with one of her company's team members and he learned how to self-publish. More importantly, he realized that other people may want the same so he started creating a program. The ability for him to discover that it's not what people want but it's what they value was priceless. He learned to help create the demand. He realized it's not about getting to the mountain top, it's about the journey to the top. Not everything goes as planned but when you work extremely hard and surround yourself around people you want to be like, there habits and mindset will rub off on you. When a 'whisper' comes into your life, don't think about it, just do it.

With some of his newfound success, Haris started being recognized. Haris' vision has become a reality. He was officially the moderator for Kevin Harrington and would break history, becoming the first student moderator to induct someone into the Hall of Fame! He was showing up at a new level. Others weren't associating with him as a peer but they were looking to him as a leader. Haris was going over his notes and getting ready to moderate and break history when he heard his name being called. Everyone was clapping and when he realized it was for him, everything shifted. Oblivious because he wasn't expecting anything,

Haris was announced as a runner up for "Entrepreneur of the Year." This was the largest college entrepreneurial event in the nation and ranked by Forbes as one of the top 5 "can't miss events" of 2015. That unexpected accomplishment came full circle. He was chasing after one of his desired mentors, eventually moderated for him and then was sharing the stage with him. Haris's vision never changed along the way and it became a reality. Haris learned that when you give and truly expect nothing back, everything you have wanted will come true. Help anyone and everyone you can and the universe will get you exactly what you ask for.

When we hear a whisper and take the first step, and then another step and then another, that movement creates momentum. And that momentum allows others to believe in themselves. And soon, a follower becomes a leader and can guide others to their Kairos moment – the moment where everything happens all at once as a result of taking a leap of faith and doing the right things by connecting with people who can open doors for you.Many discover throughout their journey that as we create success for ourselves through hard work, we eventually turn our desire to help others. A shift that can change the world. Haris did just that and his newfound dreams became to retire his parents, buy his mother a jeep and father a Porsche, a gigantic house for them and to build a six figure business by the time he is 23!

He became so focused on these goals and became crystal clear about what he wanted. He trusts that the universe will align anyone to support them in accomplishing those goals. Haris continued on his journey of surrounding himself with the right connections; people who thought differently than the majority. While they were the minority, they were the people he wanted to be around because they had the results he wanted. While attending another powerful event, Secret Knock, Haris had the opportunity to meet Les Brown, one of the world's greatest motivational speakers. Haris walked tall during that event. He had learned how to connect with people. Haris approached Les, without knowing him but knowing of him, and asked "How did it feel?" Les looked at him with his jolly, loving smile and responded, "How did what feel young man?" "Buying your mom a mansion," Haris exclaimed. Les, humbled and appreciative, admitted, "It felt great. But it wasn't about the money. It was about the impact. It was about doing something big for someone you love so much." At that moment, realizing he would always find a way, Haris wanted to create a bigger impact. Soon, he would he be granted the opportunity to get into the Fast Lane!!!

Haris was seeking the right company to align with to create a global impression. He became the Vice President of Changing Lanes International, a company focused on helping entrepreneurs make a shift, take their lives into overdrive and accelerate their dreams. He was now in the driver's seat of his future! With all of his tangible and intangible assets, he helped take Changing Lanes International to a 6-figure business within the first year and is continuing to drive forward to elevate it to a 7-figure business.

Continuing to always improve, always connect, and always contribute to the world, Haris recognized that the purpose of Changing Lanes was to help their clients gain more Recognition, more AUTHORity and create more contribution to the world through collaboration. He continued creating joint venture partnerships. Because he dominates everything, follows his whisper and serves his clients unconditionally, Haris was awarded the opportunity for a 2-month internship with Gary Vaynerchuk, a leading entrepreneur, investor, best-selling author, international keynote speaker and internet personality.

Gary has built Wine Library to become a $60+ million company and VaynerMedia to a $100+ million company with over 700 employees and international offices! Haris played a vital role in building his brand and running paid media for Gary. They are the top 1% users on Facebook. Because of Haris' skill set, the videos he has created have been shared with people that have over 130k followers, was personally featured in videos that collectively reached over 1.5 million people and created videos that cumulatively received over 4.4 million views.

Throughout his career, despite only being 22, Haris continues be a champion. He understands the road to success is always under construction. The same holds true for the transformation to his health and body. This is no small change – it's tearing down the old self and creating the new. Again, understanding to become the best you must learn from and align with the best, he began training alongside his team at Premier Combat Center. The coaches include Ryan Jensen, who is a UFC, Bellator and Strike Force veteran, Kurt Podany who competed all around the world in Muay Thai, Jose Campos and Tony Souza (who grew up with all of the Gracie's and is a 3rd degree black belt). When he traveled, he realized he needed to keep training with the best and trained with Renzo Gracie, Matt Serra, Nate Diaz and at camps like Jackson's MMA, who have some of the best fighters on the planet such as Jon Jones and Holly Holm.

Get around and stay around people who are better than you in everything you do. Mixed Martial Arts has not only become his passion but a way of life for Haris. "MMA changed my life. It has made me a better person, it has made me tougher, more confident and built my mental toughness," Haris commands. Haris recalls his first day at the gym, there was a guy inside the boxing ring and asked Haris to help him in sparring. Haris did just that and got beat up badly. He couldn't close his jaw for 2 and a half weeks. Turns out, Marcus Sursa and was the 22nd best light heavyweight on the planet. Several weeks after, he trained against Chris Leben, who is a UFC Hall of Famer. Again, Haris got beat badly but his relentlessness kept going. In life and business, we are told to always get up. Haris literally had to keep getting up after getting knocked down. He realized that if he could take that punishment and still be able to get up and move forward, nothing can stop him.

That's the approach you need in business, instead of saying why me, say try me! Life and business are one big competition. We have to battle stress, the challenges of building a business, the haters who doubt us along the way, self-doubt and disbelief in our abilities, setbacks and roadblocks that prevent us from a smooth ride to greatness, and so many other factors that determine our results. The greater the change, the greater the joy.

Competing is the most exciting thing. There is nothing more exhilarating than a huge adrenaline rush instantly reconditioning your mindset to be unstoppable. When you have trained your butt off and your team is counting on you, the bell sounds and attack. When fighting, you have one primary focus - the person across from you. That's your only focus. You're not worried about bills, girlfriends, school or anything else. You have one concern, the person across from you is wanting to take everything you worked for. The mentality you need to fight is "kill or be killed." This is the same mentality you need in business to succeed. In entrepreneurship we give up the 9-5 in exchange for grinding however many hours it takes to accomplish our mission. We must work like there is someone working 24 hours a day to take it from us. There are times when life knocks you down. As we know, it's not how many times we get knocked down but how many times we get back up that counts.

When Haris began his journey he had no connections in the personal development industry. Now, he's positioned himself as an expert and a person of influence and a leader. By following his heart and leading with passion, he's created a platform to empower others. Dedicated to making an impact, he wants to encourage others to follow their 'whispers.' More important than focusing on his limitations, he's focusing on surrounding himself with people that help him appreciate his gifts. He believes the best way to get into the Fast Lane is getting in the HOV Lane and driving the world forward together. The people in your vehicle on the road of life determine your success. He reminds himself you must "make it a priority rather than making excuses."

He believes that in order to succeed, you must get rid of all excuses first. One must believe in what they want and visualize it often. If you speak it and visualize it, it will happen. When you are not sure what to do next, seek more counsel and follow the 'whispers' only meant for you. Stay in your lane.  He realizes that if you want to be outstanding you have to be willing to stand out. Success comes from doing what others won't to separate yourself, yet not make it about yourself. Getting crystal clear about what you want and focusing on it every day increases the desire to succeed. When you serve others and do things to better yourself consistently, you become a person of value. Then you lead others to follow their "whispers" and connect the dots along the road of life to help lead them to their fastest lane to success.

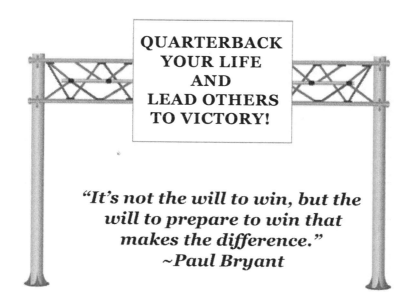

**QUARTERBACK YOUR LIFE AND LEAD OTHERS TO VICTORY!**

*"It's not the will to win, but the will to prepare to win that makes the difference."*
*~Paul Bryant*

# Jeff Garcia

The game of life has players and spectators. It's easy for those watching from the bleachers to judge and criticize those who are actually playing. However, the true players, those that are living life inside the sidelines in the game of life, grinding and creating results, are the ones who deserve all the applause. They don't deserve ovations just for the attainments they produce, but merely for the fact that they are willing to put it all on the line every day, to drive toward their goals. We learn as much in our victories as we do in our defeats and the times in our lives when we experience losses are truly the moments that define who we become.

Jeff Garcia, a small, red-headed, skinny boy raised in Gilroy, California was one of 7 siblings. If you were to judge him by appearance growing up, you may believe that his stature wouldn't allow him to accomplish as much as he did in one of the most elite and illustrious organizations in the entire world. Yet, when you discover who he truly is and the qualities he naturally possesses along with those built over the years through his experiences, you begin to understand why his professional football accomplishments pale in comparison to the quality of person he is. Jeff was a CFL Grey Cup Champion and 4-time NFL Pro Bowl quarterback, who was the NFC Passing Yards Leader one season over a 12-year career, and one of only ten quarterbacks in history to achieve two consecutive 30-touchdown passing seasons.

Yet, the trophies he hoisted over his head don't match the medals he should have for the person he represents for his family and community. When leading a team to victory on the field, there are inevitably hitches before any triumphs. The same is true off the field and Jeff learned this early on as a child experiencing some of the most difficult trials anyone could go through. The road of life is full of twists and turns and we all go through some form of adversities that make us question everything about our lives. Jeff's biggest hardship came when he was 7 years old, when he lost his best friend, his brother Jason, in a drowning accident during a Memorial Day weekend camping trip with his family.  Feeling responsible as the older brother, Jeff began to question his position on this planet and what that meant.

Just over a year later, Jeff's younger sister Kimberly, died in a tragic accident on their father's birthday. Riding in the back of a tractor for the family business, the truck hit a bump and the tailgate opened forcing her to fall out. She suffered injuries to her head and wasn't able to recover.

These incomprehensible traumas opened Jeff's eyes to how precious life truly is and how it can be taken in a heartbeat, a single breath, but it also made him want to become better. It made him want to do things for his family that wouldn't disappoint them any more than they already were. He took on the responsibility to create success in order to serve as a distraction for his parents rather than focusing on the tragic experiences they had been through. Significant flashes in time throughout life force us reflect on our relevance. Heart-wrenching losses fill our hearts with love for the ones we do have in our lives. When things happen to you as a boy they make you want to become a better man. Ultimately, when you don't know how to cope with death, the best thing you can do is truly live!

When life's hardships knock you down and the obvious option is to give up and give in, those moments when you question God and simply cannot comprehend the purpose and meaning behind why tragedies happen, the experiences you go through that you wouldn't wish upon your worst enemy, that is when you turn challenges into a Lane Change. Do not let your burdens limit you from being a driving force in the world. Turn them into momentous opportunities to become who you need for those around you and those who need you. Since that instrumental time in his life, Jeff has always turned negatives into positives.

When life pushes you back it's setting you up to make a comeback. Like a quarterback who drop steps in order to allow time for him to survey the field, there are times in life when we get pushed back and it gives us time to reflect and survey the future. The trials and tribulations help us determine what lane we want to take in order to maximize life and live it to the fullest. Often, it's the other people in our lives who can influence us and help motivate us to keep going before we become the person that others leverage to do the same. Jeff's dad, Bobby, a college football coach, one of the best motivators and the ultimate at bringing out the best in people, inspired hundreds of young men to be better people, to reach higher, to never settle for average and encouraged them to accomplish the impossible. Jeff grew up surrounded with inspiration and positivity, learning vicariously through his father's coaching.

Jeff understood the power of leadership by watching his dad and recognized it is the ability to get someone to do something they didn't realize they were capable of achieving. Jeff's father was a dynamic leader throughout his life and Jeff took on that role in his life on and off the field. His mother, who was present in Jeff's life every day, was also the daughter of a father who was a former football player and coach. Thanks to his parents, Jeff learned so much and adopted qualities evident throughout their lives that supported his journey to accomplish so much. As Jeff continued to pursue his dreams, the undue pressure on his shoulders from the deaths of his siblings, and the drive to put a smile on his parent's face, motivated him to prove his belonging. "Whatever challenges would come up in front of me were nothing compared to what I went through as a child. I was willing and wanting to meet them head on and prove people wrong, and drive through it and drive past it, not be denied and whatever it took to will my way was burning deep inside of me," Jeff boldly proclaims.

Ultimately, despite all of the other positive traits Jeff possesses, it's his work ethic, drive and commitment to excellence that fuel his success. His heritage, the son of full-blooded Mexican immigrants, instilled in Jeff those keys to becoming a genuine champion. For generations they earned their living in the fields picking whatever was in season. Grueling work day in and day out, committed to providing for their family, they never complained but took advantage of the harvest and lived fruitfully because of their labor. "There is no gain without pain and pain is temporary. And gain is something you'll live with forever," Jeff acknowledges.

The common theme amongst winners, in any area of life, is unwavering commitment and the ability to do whatever it takes become who you need to succeed when it counts. Demonstrating and showcasing that you're willing to commit yourself to the best that you can be and be willing to do it yourself is key. Conditioning yourself mentally and physically when nobody is looking is what prepares you to illustrate the skills you've gained, the mental fortitude you've developed and the dedication to win when everyone is watching. The best way to command attention from others is to command the best from yourself.

Truth be told, we all have times where we truly cannot visualize ourselves on the grand stage. Setting goals and dreaming are paramount in actually getting to hoist a trophy over your head, but the key to getting into the fast lane, is the be realistic and grounded and make the most of every moment we have at the present time. Over time, this will lead us down the right lane on the road to success. "The best thing I've done is maximize my potential in that moment and allowing that to lead to the next opportunity. You're not going to get opportunities put in front of you without creating those doors that start to crack open. You have to be ready and prepared to blow it open," professes Jeff. The reality is that we don't get the chance to play at the highest level in the world without living at the highest level in our own lives in every aspect, every single day. There are people who go through life who have opportunity after opportunity in front of them and don't take advantage of it and maximize the chance. Life's successes intersect where preparation meets opportunity.

Jeff, leading teams to victories, understands that often the best place to start when making a lane change is to surround yourself with people who will support you and help steer you in the right direction. You cannot change the people around you but you can change the people you choose to be around. "Sometimes we need someone to push us that extra mile," Jeff implores! Like an NFL Playbook or a driver's manual, throughout the road of life you begin to create your own success formula that will afford you your own blessings and achievements. The reality is that successful people do what unsuccessful people aren't willing to do. That's why those who live lives others won't ever experience are willing to do the things necessary to afford themselves experiences others cannot afford.

Sometimes in life, when it forces you to question your purpose and your potential, you may have to audible while remaining accountable to yourself and your actions. You must hold others accountable to your standards, and change who you are in order to stay the course and drive your dreams forward. Finding peace in your path helps you find purpose in your progression. Perhaps, as illustrated by Jeff in everything he's done throughout his life, being opportunistic and having perpetual positive energy in times when most would be anything but, is what allows him to get into the right lane and put himself in the position for continual victory. Defining moments, ones that you want to bottle and keep with you forever, provide us the hope and refreshing reminders that we are capable of things beyond even our imagination. And we can't win the championship without throwing our first pass.

Jeff got his start in his football career with the Calgary Stampeders in the Canadian Football League by barely making the team, fighting to be the third-string quarterback. During Jeff's 4th season he had a season-ending knee injury which forced him to work harder than ever to recover and comeback ready to compete again. His belief in becoming an NFL player had subsided and was seemingly elusive. Until he had a season to remember.

During his 5<sup>th</sup> season, one that proved life changing, was his comeback from the set back. When it came down to crunch time at the end of the season, Jeff's team didn't fail at the most key times. They took advantage of every opportunity, collectively, setting out to accomplish the goal they had set at the beginning of the year. Remembering hoisting the Grey Cup over his head with his teammates that season, Jeff values the CFL championship as one of his greatest moments during his renowned sports career. Part of it was because of the triumph and partly because of where that momentous accomplishment lead Jeff.

"Whether it's in business, or in sports of whatever activity you're taking part in, generally there is a winner at the end. There is a success story at the end. What are you willing to do and put together and bring together from a team concept and contribute yourself, being accountable yourself, to bring the necessary pieces to that puzzle, to make it all fit and all work and create that championship experience?" When we continue grinding and continue putting the pedal to the medal, redefining ourselves to truly succeed, and exceeding the expectations, it will open opportunities for what's next in your life. Success attracts opportunities.

Jeff's eyes and heart opened to the possibility of becoming an NFL quarterback. Despite being a college all-star and a Grey Cup MVP, nobody wanted to draft Jeff. Five teams were interested but zero teams wanted to officially sign him as a free agent. Yet, Bill Walsh, one of the greatest coaches in NFL history, was making calls on Jeff's behalf and fought for him the entire process. He was drafted by the San Francisco 49ers. Bill, along with the San Francisco 49ers, gave Jeff the chance to get to the next level and his childhood dream was no longer a fantasy, but a reality. Jeff's driving force became to prove Bill right about what he saw in his potential and abilities to be a winner. A 3-time Pro Bowler going into his 4<sup>th</sup> season, Jeff had proven himself and Bill that he deserved to be in that position.

Heading into the 2002 season, in an NFC wild card game against the New York Giants, one that started out great for Jeff and his team, quickly fizzled and they found themselves down 24 points midway through the 3rd quarter. When others believed it was an insurmountable lead to overcome, Jeff remembered back to his accomplishments and reminded himself and the team that it was possible. "We didn't look at having to overcome 24 points. We looked at the fact that we had to have one play at a time that would lead to consecutive plays which would lead to success. We had to worry about putting a drive together. We couldn't worry about what would happen at the end of the game. We had to focus on what we could do with every minute that we had. If we can do this as a team and handle what we need individually, and bring it all together, there is a chance we could make this happen," Jeff proudly remembers.

With one of the most memorable endings, a game touted as one of the greatest comebacks in NFL history, Jeff lead his team to a tremendously triumphant victory. The exhilaration with his team in front of the home crowd fans and the celebration in the locker room with the coaches and staff, through the blood, sweat and tears, Jeff recognizes how precious that experience was for him and the organization. In life, you can comeback from anything if you come to terms with the reality that you need to accomplish what you can step by step, play by play, day by day. When you're not given everything, you have to give everything you've got!!

Through the pursuit of excellence and proving to himself that he belonged, Jeff understands the best way to not get discouraged is to continue having courage, and encouraging others to become the greatest reflections of themselves. "A driving force for me was the opportunity to not just do great things on the field but to be able to do great things off the field. I wanted to be a great giver in life. I've been put on this earth to give back and be put in a position to lift others up and to support and help others to find a way to succeed and have a chance in life." Jeff has achieved some of the most desirable accomplishments in a sports-figures' career. And yet, with how thrilled he is to have achieved them, he seems to be most proud about how he's helping people truly win at life off the field. His foundation, the Garcia Pass It On Foundation, teams up with great organizations like the Hispanic Scholarship Fund, to create financial support for Hispanic students who want to pursue a college education.

Perhaps, in life, it's not about passing a game-winning touchdown but it's about passing on hope and dreams for those around us. Perhaps it's not about handing the ball off to your running back to run it in the end zone but it's about handing your wisdom and guidance to kids who need some direction and love. Perhaps it's not about tackling the wide receiver on the field but it's about tackling key issues in the lives of mislead youth. A true champion makes those around him their best. His continual pursuit of excellence inspires others to accomplish more. "If you're not striving, if you're not driving and you're not trying to pursue excellence in your own life in some sort of way, then you're wasting your life." We have one opportunity to live and we don't know the play clock in the game of life. It's time to make a shift. It's time to take everything you're doing and make a Lane Change. It's time to accelerate your dreams.

When is the last time you did something for the first time? Is it possible that today you'll do a first and not realize it will be your last? You don't live life, you create one. Imagine living every day of your life as if it's your 2-minute drill. It's your time to bring it all together. It's your time to take the trials and tribulations you've suffered and use them as motivation by parlaying them with your victories and triumphs to put all you've got on the line. Imagine giving everything you've got for everyone around you and proving yourself right. Can you imagine how different your life would be if you lived every day as if it were your Super Bowl? Good, because it IS your moment. The clock is ticking. It's time to quarterback your life, draw up a winning drive and take your life into the fast lane!

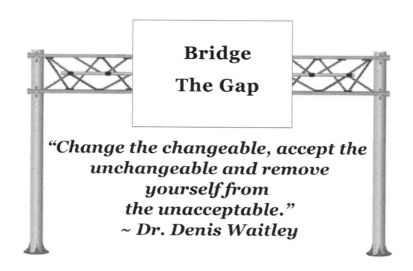

## Bridge
## The Gap

*"Change the changeable, accept the unchangeable and remove yourself from the unacceptable."*
*~ Dr. Denis Waitley*

# Jeff Hoffman

Jeff Hoffman is a world-leading entrepreneur with a vision that supersedes money and pays a far bigger dividend. Over the course of his career he has launched some of the most well-known start-up companies, and what began as a means to end turned into a new beginning that is changing the world. Entrepreneurship for Jeff, like many, started unintentionally because he had a problem he couldn't solve; he wanted to attend a college he couldn't afford. Through scholarships and financial aid, he was able to attend but through lack of funds he was told to go home. And the average person would have. And the average entrepreneur when faced with a challenge quits too. But Jeff realized if he listened to everyone telling him to drop out and quit, that would have set his standard for the future.

As a freshman, Jeff started his first company simply to be able to fund his goal of receiving a college diploma. The real lesson was learned outside of academia. He quickly learned that if you have a hard problem to solve and nobody else to help you solve it, entrepreneurship and start-ups can serve as a great means to an end. Throughout school we are taught a lesson and then given the test. In life, we are given a test and have to decipher the lesson. And along the traditional path, somebody's unwritten rule book dictates that we should go to school, get a degree that can serve the purpose of getting a job at good company. And Jeff did just that. Yet he hated every day of his corporate job because of the bureaucracy, the politics and the heavy overhead of constantly having to please management and not customers. Like many, frustrated and challenged, Jeff simply wanted control of his own destiny. He needed a lane change.

He realized that entrepreneurship was the vehicle that would open new lanes to freedom and self-determination. It was never about the money; it was about the choices he wanted to be able to design his own life. Jeff discerns that the difference between entrepreneurs and everybody else is how we handle our problems. Recognizing that we all encounter difficulties in the world, entrepreneurs observe the problem and determine if it's bothering anybody else. If the answer is yes, they do research to determine if there is already a solution to the problem. And finally, if there is not a viable answer, they figure out the solution with a determinant attitude that they are the one who should be the solution to the problem. "Inefficiency makes me nuts," Jeff recognizes, "and I have a singular focus of resolving a problem and I won't sleep until that thing is fixed."

Jeff also recognizes that it's not a one-lane road. Each of us has something we do really well, but it's paramount to surround yourself with people who are smarter than you in the areas that you're weakest in. Jeff believes that while most people purport that the biggest need for start-ups is funding, talent is much more scarce than money. He puts such a huge emphasis on networking and encourages entrepreneurs to always be searching for new talent to create collaboration. The strength of your network determines the strength of your team. And if you start searching for someone when you need them, you're already too far behind.

And sometimes within a company, there may need to be a change of roles to maximize the efficiency of the mission. While you may be educated in a particular niche, it may be a reality that there is someone within the company that is better than you. Jeff remembers first hand, while acting as the CEO, being called out and asked to change his contribution to the company. While his degree was in computer science and programming, the best role for Jeff was not programming because he wasn't the most proficient. And while that doesn't make you obsolete, it certainly makes you less impactful than that team member.

Ego aside, Jeff realized that in order to contribute the greatest to the overall mission, his role would be better for the company in marketing. While he didn't know marketing, he did research by interviewing marketers. He realized that they couldn't understand the engineering and technology side while the engineers couldn't communicate with the marketers in business terms. This was pivotal moment for Jeff, creating his most impactful lane change as an entrepreneur. He recognized a gap. Some people in his company were in the far left lane and some people were in the far right lane and nobody was in the center lane. Jeff made a shift and bridged the gap, creating a new position within the company and was able to drive the entire company forward and his career went into overdrive.

As a result of this radical shift, Jeff believes in both competition and collaboration. As a founder of Priceline.com and uBid.com, among others, he appreciates that there are components within a company where another company may be able to come alongside and collaborate. There could also be components within the same joint venture that competition will birth the best product. And even more possible is the idea that competitive collaboration will produce more wins for both companies. Along the journey of self-discovery through building businesses, Jeff proposes that entrepreneurs are both born and made. There are a whole set of skills, tools, techniques and experiences that can be learned. There are also a lot of people who have made many mistakes and learned a lot of the lessons who can mentor you. That would suggest that anyone can become a successful entrepreneur. That said, fundamentally, there is a different mindset that determines the risk profile of someone and their ability, through unfiltered thinking, to create a solution from a problem.

Entrepreneurs thrive on uncertainty because it is an opportunity that stimulates them to get creative. 'Necessity is the mother of invention' and perhaps we could now suggest that 'uncertainty is the daddy of discovery and development.' We find ourselves in an economic time that is fostering that need and desire for entrepreneurs. Through circumstance, people are discovering abilities they didn't tap into in order to create opportunities that aren't presently possible for them. Moreover, because of the huge tsunami of entrepreneurship, more opportunities are being created for people to evolve into entrepreneurs and adapt accordingly to create a new reality.

"Entrepreneurship is a privilege, not a job" Jeff suggests. The adventure that one goes on when choosing to accept the opportunity is more important than the money that comes with the success. Dreams can come true because of entrepreneurship. And entrepreneurs can also, more importantly, help the dreams of others become reality. Jeff has transitioned from launching companies, to launching entrepreneurs who go launch new companies.

The dollar that can be made by starting another company is not nearly as impactful as the difference that can be made by equipping an army of entrepreneurs to go change the world.

Jeff determines who he wants to mentor based on their ability to scale and their amount of influence to pay it forward. When he believes that an entrepreneur will make a difference in the world based on their mission, he's more passionate about supporting their dreams. As one of the founders of Priceline.com, Jeff admits that his passion for travel is really spawned by his love of people. He recognizes that the happiness index of a country is more important than the landmarks it can offer. His desire to learn about a country and its culture, along with the places where there is the most change in the air, are the places he loves visiting.

As the landscape of our world changes, so does that landscape of entrepreneurship. And so too, does that landscape of a man who has built some of the biggest companies that have shaped our world. When you get to enjoy the blessings that come with the hard work of finding a problem and creating a solution, life and business become more about the people behind the companies and the hearts and souls behind the vision. Entrepreneurship is the vehicle that can provide the solutions to the world's biggest challenges such as strife, war, political unrest and poverty. When you have nothing to lose and nothing to live for we resort to caring less about people. When you can teach others how to help themselves so they can create a better life, we can fundamentally resolve some of those conflicts.

Jeff is driven by the desire to show as many people the components of entrepreneurship. This will help create resolve in their own life so collectively we can resolve some of the biggest challenges we are facing throughout our world today. If we stay in the slow lane, we will stay stuck in a slow worldly demise. If we want to create a radical shift in the direction of our world, we need to get in the fast lane and pave the way via the road to entrepreneurship.

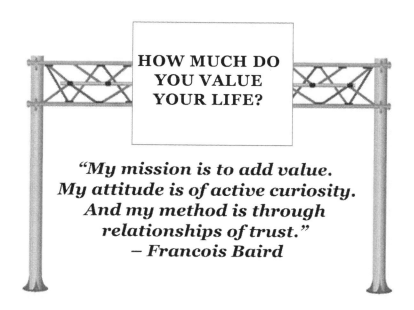

"*My mission is to add value.*
*My attitude is of active curiosity.*
*And my method is through*
*relationships of trust.*"
*– Francois Baird*

## John Lee Dumas

John Lee Dumas, a son of a military father who went on to run his own law practice, admired his father for his service to our country as well as the entrepreneurial route he took after, building his own small business. Believing that was his path to success also, at age 17 John decided to look into ROTC and apply for a scholarship, which was an intense process to get accepted. Upon receiving the acceptance letter from Providence College, he realized that this was a game changing moment and that anything worth having is worth working for.

At a fork in the road, he had to determine if he wanted to travel the lane that could lead him to where the majority of college students go, or the lane that would lead him to a life of discipline and regimented focus that would be imposed upon him through military training. He took the road less traveled and it made all the difference. Over the next 12 years, 4 in college and 8 serving as an Army Officer, John was building a solid foundation that would assist him throughout his entrepreneurial career in civilian life.

Reflecting back on his experience, John attributes much of his success to the lessons he learned during his tenure. In the military they are taught a lesson and then put through the ultimate test, sometimes at the risk of their lives. In life, we are given tests and must determine the lesson. The number one principle John incorporated into his business that he learned from the military was the importance of systems and automation. When he was pinned as a second lieutenant, arriving at his first duty station as a 22-year old, he was in charge of many lives of his fellow soldiers in the combat arms brand division. When he took over the platoon, they were six months from deploying to Iraq.

Realizing that the preparation it would take to get everything accomplished according to the training schedule was potentially unattainable, John understood that it would remain that way without systems and automation in place. As one person leading a group of men, he realized he needed to leverage his time and scale his entire platoon's training to the level necessary in order to be adequately prepared for their deployment.

We often overlook the importance of setting goals with timelines because we hope that the results will show up. The reality is our businesses rise and fall on leadership and structure. As entrepreneurs, we often don't deploy the things we need in our businesses in order to fight the fight and survive the business world. And while our lives may not be at risk like John's was serving overseas, our livelihood certainly is based on our businesses daily operations.

Through the journey of becoming a significant influencer in the business world, John discovered that education can make you a living while self-education can make you a fortune. Reading business and finance books constantly, listening to personal development audios continually, John understood that to become the best, he needed to learn from the best. Reading a quote that would later become more treasured because of its worth, Albert Einstein suggested "Try not to become a person of success, but rather a person of value."

When John read this at age 26 he didn't absorb it completely and continued to pursue personal achievements. Over the course of the next 6 years, John's lane of choice was personal satisfaction which ended down lonely road of unhappiness and dissatisfaction. Yet, still working on himself habitually, he came across the powerful commendation from Einstein again and this time it went from his head to his heart, transforming his paradigm and fueling his passion for helping others. "What if I just become a person of value? What if I create free, valuable and consistent content?" John pondered.

That was the birth of his future, a movement that is wonderfully empowering individuals around the world to pursue their aspirations and accomplish their goals. Running the world's leading business PODCAST, John Lee Dumas is the


P roducer

O f

D reams;

C hanging lives

And

S etting the Standard

T oday

 Putting other people before himself and their desires in front of his own, removing money as the target goal and transforming his mind from chasing money to pursuing value for others, John now considers happiness to be the noteworthy mile marker. John changed lanes by accelerating everything in direct relation to the value he was able to provide to the marketplace. Straightforwardly, the man who does more than he is paid for will soon be paid for more than he does. Entrepreneur on Fire was spawned out of the desire to have a 7-day podcast with valuable content as a consumer, which didn't exist at the time.

 With the vision of creating what he wanted, understanding others undoubtedly wanted the same, John simply created a solution for a problem. Since the inception, John's vision remains focused on providing value. With over 1400 episodes, over 1.5 million listens per month in 145 countries, producing over 7 figures, Entrepreneur on Fire is creating embers that are sparking others to fuel their dreams as they set the world on fire, trailblazing a like-minded community because of John's vision.

 John continues to ignite his movement by driving the world forward with a focused mission. The key to his success is helping others move from being busy to being productive. He attributes much of his success to the process and foundation upon which he builds each day. With intentional desire, John's results are tracked publicly through monthly income reports. He has implemented what he preaches and intently believes transparency is key in creating trust with your tribe.

Daily, John encourages Fire Nation to always be growing toward the plan they have created. Be decisive. Right or wrong, make a decision. The road of life is paved with flat squirrels who couldn't make a decision. Each of us has the same amount of time and yet on a score card, most people don't live up to their intentions because their actions don't correspond accordingly. Everybody wants to be a diamond but very few are willing to get cut. Many want to be on fire but most are not willing to get burned. In the end, direction is so much more important than speed; many are going nowhere fast. If you are unclear, attempt this: When you get to the end of the day, what are you unwilling to say you have not done? Do those things. First. Now.

The Freedom Journal was designed by John in order to guide you in accomplishing your #1 goal in 100 days through a unique step-by-step process. Successful entrepreneurs know how to identify and set one big goal at a time and then execute effectively on that goal. Most entrepreneurs fail because they don't have accountability. This unique support system is the solution because it bridges the gap between those who want to create results and those who are. If you're ready to crush your highest business priority in 100 days, the Freedom Journal will guide you there and knock over that one big domino to start a chain reaction of massive success in your life!

Fire Nation is sweeping the world because of a united undertaking with a universal passion for one cause. The ripple effect from everything around Fire Nation is creating an impact on people around the globe. Sky above me. Earth below me. Fire within me. The Fire Nation cloud of smoke billowing from the fires created inside of individual entrepreneurs around the world is growing and continues to be fueled by their dreams and successes. What fires you up? Where can you add more value to others?

The road to success is driven by you. The lane you choose to take can lead to opportunities you cannot imagine. The driving force must be to contribute to the world in a way that provides so much value that even when you're on cruise control, those who follow you can draft off your forward momentum. The road to your greatest starts by helping others get on the road to theirs. Leaders who focus on what Fire Nation promotes will get into the fast lane and pave new roads for others to follow on the way to their most fulfilled life. The road to success is always under construction. It's time to turn up the heat and join the Fire Nation movement – perhaps at that point you can be in the Fire Lane and the Fast Lane at the same time!

## HERE'S THE WINDUP, AND THE PITCH!

*"The important thing is not to stop questioning. Curiosity has its own reason for existing."*
*~Albert Einstein*

# Kevin Harrington

Kevin Harrington has become a household name mostly by bringing a multitude of products from the marketplace into your home. The reality is that his success has come from taking advantage of life-changing experiences, seizing them and turning them into opportunities for others to create success. As one of the most successful entrepreneurs of our time, Kevin Harrington has taken over 500 products and businesses to the next level, generating more than $5 Billion in sales worldwide. And yet to reach this success, like all aspiring entrepreneurs, he had to start somewhere.

Kevin had the desire to own his own business and be an entrepreneur from a young age. And he understood that there is almost no such thing as ready. There is only now and as all successful business people understand, especially those who get into the fast lane, that now is as good a time as any. Grasping this concept, he began exposing himself and his persona to as many opportunities as possible. He entered what he calls the 'Curiosity Overload' phase in which he was on an exploration to figure out what he loved and where he could excel. "In life you have to present yourself and you have to focus on exposing yourself to more opportunities. The more opportunities you have, the bigger and better you can grow and build as an entrepreneur," Kevin adopts as a core principle.

Understanding he needed to acquire business savvy, at age 20, Kevin decided he would start a business brokerage business. While he didn't know everything he needed to create success, this endeavor forced him to comprehend the inner workings of dynamic businesses – why they were selling, why they were growing, why they were struggling and overall how these companies operated. Ultimately, Kevin uncovered key components that would later make him a fortune. "I was exposing myself through this 'curiosity overload' to many opportunities so that I knew when the right one came along that it was going to smack me in the face and send me the right direction."

Often, on the road of life we believe that we can just coast and it will all work out. If you don't know where you're going any road will get you there. Instead, professional entrepreneurs know that when we want to work things out in our favor, we pave the right lane for us and drive the world forward.

Kevin attended nearly every trade show to learn and emerge himself into the world he wanted to dominate. He would trade his time for knowledge and wisdom. When you study your competition, do what's necessary to learn the industry and do what it takes to create enough value in the marketplace, you will eventually surpass the competition. Today, Kevin continues to attend trade shows to fuel his 'curiosity overload,' stay in tune with new products and developing techniques, as well as expose himself to more opportunities and media. When we take the open road it will lead us to the best lane for us.

While Kevin was attending the Philadelphia Home Show, he observed a guy at a booth who was demonstrating the benefits of a ginsu knife, and more importantly he was successfully selling them. Observing that 9 out of 10 viewers would rush the table to purchase the knife set, the lightbulb went off. "There's a guy that knows how to sell," Kevin noticed, "what if we put him up on television so that instead of being in front of 10 people he could be in front of millions?" Kevin invested $2000 into filming that presentation and eventually it turned into a $500 million program, Kevin had helped Arnold become a huge success. Arnold, seeing an opportunity himself, introduced Kevin to other pitch guys at various trade shows in exchange for a little piece of the action.

The birth of the infomercial impregnated a new market with life-changing products and Kevin became the father of an entire new industry that he created. Those who create dream lifestyles take an opportune moment and make it a momentous opportunity for others. The power of seizing and opportunity and creating leverage will take you from the slow lane to the fast lane! Life is about seizing those moments that could change everything you know. Change is constant and our lives need to change for us to be able to understand how to change more lives. When we look out for new beginnings, our outlook will be renewed and restored.

Many view Kevin's success as being lucky. "I programmed myself to be at the right place at the right time. I wanted to be in the right lane. I wanted to be in that fast lane to success. But you need to stay in the fast lane, that game-changing lane that gives you the ability to speed right through it all." As Kevin built his empire, he actually started with the finish line first. While he didn't know what vehicle would drive him to success, he knew the destination. On the journey, there is a road map and a set of directions. The first allows you options to arrive there any possible way while the latter gives you a specific course to navigate. As a revolutionary pioneer, Kevin used a map to create his set of directions. The counsel he has developed over time in his pursuit to becoming one of the most influential investors in today's market worldwide, Kevin became one of the original panelists on the hit TV show "Shark Tank." He shares his process to create a powerful and influential pitch whether you're making the sale of a product, attracting investors or getting a promotion:

1) Start with the problem in order to gain the listener's attention
2) Solve the problem using some magical transformations and benefits in a unique fashion
3) Make an irresistible offer

The entire concept is structured to Tease, Please and then Seize!!

And while most simply talk about what it takes, Kevin continues being curious while remaining furious, continually raises his profile and programs himself to become a person of influence and continuously tests before he invests. When you get into the right lane and you're accelerating, you have the opportunity to stay at the head of your pack. In the entrepreneurial lane you need to watch out for other drivers because it's fast and furious and by continuing to innovate, you solidify yourself as a key person of influence and limit the ability of your competition to catch up. Ultimately, what drives Kevin is building a future for his family. He has no desire to slow down. Every day is a new day to impact people's lives and help them achieve their dreams. "My eyes are visualizing what's happening through their eyes and it's an opportunity for me to help them get in the fast lane. Some people are chugging along at 25 MPH and if they just had my vision, they would move over into the fast lane and get there a lot faster," Kevin confirms.

At the end of the day, the things that happen to us are not as important as our attitude and perspective about those momentous opportunities in our lives. Life is about seizing those moments that could change everything you know. Yours will be marked by extraordinary defeats and even more extraordinary accomplishments. Those who create massive success take an opportune moment, seize the opportunity and make it a momentous opportunity for others. Then they take it into overdrive and accelerate their contribution to the world.

LIFE TAKES A LOT
OF (PAINT) BALLS!

"To Hell with circumstances;
I create opportunities."
-Bruce Lee

# Mark Lack

Where most seek peace and serenity, Mark Lack reveled in an environment where he was constantly under attack. From an early age, he chose to engage himself in a system that thrived on hiding to be safe, while putting himself in vulnerable situations, literally sticking his neck out to advance himself into more strategic positions. SPLAT!

Mark got to literally paint his future. But it wasn't with brushstrokes on a canvas, it was actually with constant brushes with danger on a battlefield! At age 14, Mark became infatuated with Professional Paintball. Knowing he had been a quitter, giving up every hobby to that point and lacking true discipline to see things through, he had to convince his parents to purchase him the expensive equipment. Influencing them to trust that he would actually follow through, his loving, supporting parents obliged after much persistence from Mark, a characteristic that would serve him well throughout his careers.

From 14-18, Mark was a teammate on the best team in the world, Team Dynasty, and traveled over 250,000 miles around the globe competing professionally. He won over $300,000 in cash prizes in high school alone. Yet, the trophies he won would never match up to the victories he learned about himself and the "science of achievement" from fellow professionals who competed at the highest level. "When you truly get into a Lane that you're passionate about, you can go anywhere. You can be the best in the world, but you are not going to achieve the success you want until you are in a Lane that you are extremely obsessive about," Mark emphasizes. The mindset, the principles and the foundation that the best of the best embody is congruent in any endeavor.

The courses he played professional paintball were always level playing fields for both teams. The advantage went to the team who had the understanding that the game was actually played in the mind more than in the flesh. In life and in business, we often need to strategically work with teams to survive and thrive. Yet often, different from his teammates who strategically hid behind bunkers for protection, entrepreneurs find themselves cowering behind their perceptive fears they believe are protecting them when, in actuality, they are making them vulnerable to settle for a life of mediocrity.

The welts on his body from being shot with paintballs hurt. The failures along the road to success will be painful too. It is the lessons learned and the accomplishments that help you forget about the pain endured along the journey. Ultimately, the man Mark wanted to become and the life he wanted to have was not going to happen by remaining in his current lane. He had to remove himself from the world he knew, where he was one of the top 20 in the entire world, and change lanes. While most take a "shot in the dark" to discover success, Mark strategically determined the course he wanted to create for himself. Having fallen in love with the science of achievement, Mark continually invested in the principles of the elite.

Watching a Tony Robbins' video, for the first time, Mark's personal check engine light illuminated and he began to tune up his vision when he heard "The fact that you alive right now, regardless of your circumstances, means that you have the moral responsibility to become your best self, and as a result of becoming your best self, experience all that the wonderful world has to offer to you. You must find a purpose to serve that's greater than yourself."

For the first time, Mark discovered that his desires to have more must shift to the desire to become more. He believes that whatever you want will be a direct reflection of who've you become and what you have given. It is a paramount principle of success to have an unwavering commitment to constantly be growing. Every professional in every industry drives their success by incessantly immersing themselves in continuing education through reading books, attending seminars, listening to audios and being part of a mastermind. The more we invest in ourselves, the more abundant we become. As the world evolves, so too, must our progress. Mark finds that those who solely focus on the Science of Achievement, while they may obtain everything they want based on societal expectations, achieving various "trophies" along the journey, it's those who focus on the Science of Fulfillment who gain the true rewards in life.

Mark, through interviewing the top achievers in the world, has adopted his set of values and beliefs based on their lives as well as the results he has achieved by implementing the strategies and tactics into his business and personal life. The distinct difference between someone who is successful and someone who continually gets flat tires on the road of life, is their ability to leverage, maximize and optimize their resourcefulness. At the expense of one's desires, by only going after money we lose sight of the wealth that can be achieved by living a fulfilled life. Where our energy goes, our life flows. There is nothing bad about compounding the art and science of achievement; it will be what allows you to gain more in order to give more. Yet, there is so much more to gain when you are driving down the art and science of fulfillment path because it leads to a better quality of life paved by love and increased consciousness.

BE more.

HAVE more.

GIVE more.

"It's not just who you become, but as you become a better version of yourself, you will naturally start to have more so you now have a responsibility to give more," Mark declares. When you want something, learn from someone who already has it at a level way above what you want to achieve. When you want to become somebody, learn from someone whose values embody what you want at a level way above you!

Mark has accomplished a lot in his life, partly because he has aligned with people who have become and have more than he did; it's also in part to the habits and practices he implements into his daily life. Being proactive rather than reactive in life is a key to becoming a Lane Changer. Our ability to condition our lives will determine the condition of our lives.

Mark has disciplined himself to create a life rather than have life create his reality. His practices that he automatically and routinely does have shaped his certainty, and he begins every morning intentionally:

- Starting with gratitude
- Drinking water with lemon to alkaline his body
- Drinking a healthy protein shake or vegetable juice smoothie
- Relaxing, spending time meditating on his vision for life, and also reflecting on how far he has come
- Reminding himself that it's about the journey, not the destination
- Reading intentionally on how to move closer to his goals or a book to recalibrate himself to become closer to the achievement of fulfillment
- Listening to John Assaraf's brain retraining program to recondition his subconscious
- Reading his affirmations

Ultimately, our beliefs about ourselves and the model of the world impact who we become. The more we control what we can, the more capacity we will have when life spirals out of control. Our ability to focus on the highest impact activities, the ability to be productive rather than simply active, and our capability to grow and expand will directly correlate to the results we attain. Our performance in our minds dictates our performance in the game of life. Like in paintball, the ammo we have in life determines our ability to aim at our target and hit our goals. Practice makes perfect only when practice makes permanence. Practice the habit, not the effort. You cannot make temporary effort and expect permanent results.

When you continually adjust your alignment, lubricate your skills, tune up your vision and shift your desire from achievement to contribution, you will accelerate your dreams. Exponentially speeding these up and compounding your relentless desire to live a fulfilled life, will help you find your lane and improve the vehicle you're using to drive the world forward. "No matter where you are in life, no matter what your circumstances are, no matter what your resources are or your access to money and knowledge, if you are committed to the vision, if you have a big enough reason why that vision must become a reality, you can achieve it. The way you will get into the fast lane is by investing your time, energy, and resources toward a commitment to becoming the person you need to become."

We have an obligation to contribute by paying it forward and adding value to others along the way. Getting into the Fast Lane is finding a purpose to serve that is greater than yourself. When you can help others along the road to your greatest life, the road to abundance opens up for everyone.

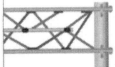

YOUR LIFE IS
EITHER
A BLOCKBUSTER
OR LACKLUSTER!

*"All our dreams can come true,
if we have the courage to pursue them."*
*~Walt Disney*

# Nik Halik

Nik Halik possesses a nearly indescribable enthusiasm and passion that exudes because of his intentional purpose of living life not just in the fast lane, but on the super highway of an extraordinary life. He epitomizes the concept of pursuing dreams and turning them into realities. And it all started with a childhood fantasy when Nik wrote the original screenplay for his life; since then he has been the actor, producer and director, making that screenplay become the movie that is his life.

At age 8, medically quarantined to his house, Nik began dreaming of all the things he wanted to do when his health improved. He didn't have a traditional formal education and developed a unique perception of academia based on his first mentors - the Encyclopedia Britannica and the world atlas. Early on, Nik discovered that entrepreneurship was the only legitimate way he was going to be able to create the life he had designed and turn his dreams into reality. He realized that most children become very conditioned to the system, thwarting their creativity. In traditional academia we get reprimanded for creativity and, as a result, as we grow older, we lose our sense of wonder.

As we enter the working world our employers and the government determine the rules which dominate our lives. Because our creativity and passion have been extinguished, we must learn to rediscover ourselves. He believes that as adults we need to remain childish in our ways by asking questions, being colorful, being creative and challenging the status quo to get whatever we want. Nik believes that we can do anything in the world as long as we recondition our minds and discover a strategy how to overcome any limitations that may prevent those results.

For everything Nik has been able to accomplish, he has used a simple process in order to turn a thought into a result. And you can also turn your thoughts into results. First you must internalize your goals, then you must emotionalize your goals and then you must socialize your goals by telling the rest of the world. With big, bold dreams, Nik needed to be able to fund his lifestyle. He internalized, emotionalized and socialized his vision. Entrepreneurship is the vehicle that affords him the ability to fulfill the screenplay he wrote for his life. He determined that he wanted to live life in the fast lane, and he uses his passions to drive his vision forward.

If you chase money, you will never have it. Instead chase your desires and as a default money will organically appear. You need to find that component of life that fuels your passion. Once you define that x-factor, take action. Help others internalize, emotionalize and then socialize their goals and dreams. Have others keep you accountable. The more value you add the more organically the world will conspire for you. At the end of the day we are measured by our contribution. The goal is to constantly value factor people's lives. By default, in proportion to the relation and the intensity of the value you add to others, the more abundant your life will become. Additionally, the more organically you will manifest abundance into your life.

"I get paid to think, I get paid to add value and I outsource the administration of my ideas to others. But ultimately, it's the experiential element of life. Every day is a magical day full of experiential living," Nik exclaims in a life-giving enthusiastic manner. The paradigm most people are living by is skewed based on the people that they learned it from. Nik believes that a lot of people die before they're buried. Nik acknowledges that there are obstacles and challenges every day. But, he embraces hurdles and loves the challenges because on the other side are the answers and opportunities. He loves smashing possibilities. He continually challenges himself and actually seeks out challenges. He approaches life with a zest that says 'bring it on' but with a confidence that says 'I will conquer anything I need to get where I want to go.'

The ability to learn about others and new cultures is something that drives him. Nik despises complacency. As he thinks about all he has accomplished, the biggest triumph hasn't happened yet. Life is a journey of self-discovery and striving for a little more every day. Nik lives by the belief that there are two rules:

Rule #1: There are not rules

Rule #2: Do not forget rule number 1


He is a non-conformist, believing that solitude is the silent teacher. Escapism is the ultimate utopia. In order to keep discovering who he is, Nik finds places to go that afford him the ability to discover more of himself. Yet as individualistic as he remains, he's always around the right people, admitting that if you're around 9 other losers you become the tenth. His mission of traveling the world in a way most only dream of has made the world know him as the "Thrillionaire." From having lunch on the Titanic at the ocean floor to conducting a HALO Skydive jump above Mt. Everest, from summiting some of the world's highest peaks to sleeping on the inside of an active volcano, from sleeping in one of the Egyptian pyramids for days to participating in a civilian edge of space flight, Nik is a trailblazer.

If you want to get in the fast lane, it's important to experience something different, observe life from a new vantage point and get a clearer vision and focus of what you truly want. Change the polarity of the circumstances by changing the polarity of your thinking. On the road of life, most individuals are following parked cars. They're stuck in a cul de sac, allowing the law of diminishing intent to drive them. They have a massive desire for a greater life and yet continue circling around in the dead end. When you want something different in your life, you must change, and it may take doing the complete opposite of everything you've done to this point in your life. Change lanes and go in an entirely new direction. And keep driving. You may pass everyone and end up on a one-lane road, but that's where you will truly discover who you are. Nik professes that "we are given one full tank of gas and I would rather die on empty." Life moves fast and if you don't live life in the fast lane on the super highway to your best life, you are going to miss everything it has to offer.

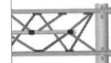

## I KNOW WHAT YOU DID THAT SUMMER

*"The beauty of a woman must be seen from in her eyes, because that is the doorway to her heart, the place where love resides."*
*— Audrey Hepburn*

# Noelle Nieporte

When you meet someone who has a love for life so passionate that as a result you become a better person, do everything in your power to surround yourself with her as much as possible. Noelle Nieporte epitomizes living in such a way; she lives for the minute and enjoys every second of it. Through her devotion to making the rest of her life the best of her life, it's not just for herself, but for everyone her heart desires to help. Noelle, a feisty spitfire who grew up in Pittsburgh, Pennsylvania in a middle-class Italian family, remembers having a good life, but always wanted a great life. "There's so much more out in the world, but I don't know what it is," she thought. "I wanted to change the world, but I had no idea what that meant."

One summer, she had the opportunity to go to California to visit family on the west coast. She had never been outside of her hometown. The challenge, however, is when we want something so bad and we have to remove ourselves from our comfort zone, the susceptibility is to remain complacent and continue doing what we know. And at those moments, perhaps those are the times we need a lane change. Often, we find ourselves with opportunities that force us to be removed from everything we know. Those experiences help us discover many things we don't know.

Noelle's uncle, an entrepreneur who owned art galleries in San Francisco, quickly taught Noelle things she wouldn't have otherwise learned if she hadn't made the decision to spend the summer there. She began selling very expensive pieces of art, but what she fell in love with was the art of running a successful business. Her uncle strongly encouraged her to get another job in addition to helping around the galleries. Noelle ended up working at Nordstrom selling clothes, and at the same time buying into the idea that she could do whatever she wanted! This job didn't just teach her about clothing, it taught her how to wear her passions on her sleeve.

Noelle discovered that she appreciated the laid-back lifestyle in California, which differed drastically from the fast-paced and overwhelming attitude and environment on the east coast. California didn't just speak to her, it helped her find her true calling. When Noelle dreams, she dreams big. Her dad, who has always supported her, convinced her to return home to complete her final year of high school. She agreed, reluctantly, but kept her vision of moving after graduation to fulfill her newfound dreams.

Her senior year, back in her home town, Noelle was crowned Miss Pennsylvania and the experiences she would have during the pageants helped shape her love of non-profits, networking, people and performing. She realized that being in front of audiences gave her the ability to influence and use her gifts to inspire others.

In addition to this exceptional honor and award her senior year, Noelle was recruited to play soccer at Penn State, which she graciously declined. As an elite soccer player and Ms. Pennsylvania, despite the bruises and cuts on her legs and the scars that were visible to the audience, Noelle's true beauty was not just in her physical appearance, but on the inside too. What Noelle would discover about herself at this point in life became a valuable asset she would use later in life to empower those closest to her, and those whom she wouldn't even meet.

After graduation, for no other reason than her cousin's suggestion, Noelle attended college in Utah. She didn't know a single soul and didn't even know where Utah was on the U.S. map. She just felt in her heart and soul that was her next move. And she was right. She met her future husband in college and Noelle, at 20 years old, quickly determined that home is where your heart is, but it's also who has your heart. Later, she realized she was driving to Utah the same day her husband was moving back to Utah. When we are at a crossroads in life, continuing to drive forward may lead us to cross roads with the people who become most important in our lives. Often, when we follow the lane designed for us, it leads us to destination that's best. When things shift, the best thing may just to embrace the change and let it happen.

Noelle allowed the changes in her life to lead them to each next phase of their lives. While she was finding her true home, she wanted to make money selling houses and began a career in real estate. The experiences of selling high-end art work and retail clothing, along with the skills she learned from her uncle the summer in California, along with all the talents she gained from being Ms. Pennsylvania, all contributed to her success in her new field. Noelle has always known what she likes, what she wants and what she loves. They may not always be the same, but together they helped her find joy in everything.

Through the ups and downs of building a business, Noelle adopted the principle that you can give a piece of your mind, but you must always give all of your heart. And this would become essential as she changed lanes from being a wife to a mother.

Ben and Noelle gave birth to their first born daughter, Rylee, who was born without a left hand. When life hands you a surprising lane change, it may actually just be an unexpected gift. As Noelle had discovered on stage with her bruised and battered shins, we can cover up the physical marks that can be seen or we can be proud and display them to the entire world. At the same time, perhaps it's more valuable to uncover those we can't see because they define who we truly are; they may become the courage others need to display their best selves to the world. Our invisible scars are often more painful than our visible ones. We all have blemishes that affect our appearance, but it's those unique deformations that truly mark who we are as a person.

A new Mompreneur, Noelle was now driven by her love of her 3 daughters. Realizing the best present was her presence, she quickly learned how to balance family life and business. When she needed to be a mom, she devoted all of herself to her family. When she was able and could devote herself to growing her businesses, she hit the pavement and got into the fast lane driving her vision forward.

When it comes to running a business, your ability to keep yourself in check will ultimately lead to more checks. The ability to remain focused and passionate is a key to getting into the fast lane. Noelle's path to higher levels of success reveals that her relentless attitude and boundless determination have been a central part of her essence since childhood. Noelle has instilled in her children exceptional work ethic and discipline to accomplish what is needed to succeed. While you may not use your college degree directly, to a large degree, college can provide experiences that teach you more than any professor. More importantly to Noelle, in her own life and as a representation to her children, she values pride in accomplishments, responsibility, continual growth as a person and accountability to being their ultimate greatest.

"I want to be the best person for me, the best example for my girls and the best representation for those who I can influence," Noelle boldly acknowledges. Through continuing to put the pedal to the metal, life will guide you toward your dreams. Your truest self will direct and guide you to your purpose. To find your right lane, it's paramount to recognize the things that appear over and over in your life. When you experience reoccurring themes in your life, pay attention. As an entrepreneur, that's when you start a business around those reoccurrences and get paid.

Like building a car, you take all the pieces and put them together to build the machine. In life, Noelle has taken all the pieces of her life and the collaboration of all of them have created the ultimate road for her to travel. Fashion is now the vehicle that Noelle uses to fuel her life. Hiding behind her stunning personality was a truly exceptional entrepreneurial mind. Her ability to rise to any occasion is prominently demonstrated by Noelle as she maintains dual roles as both the co-owner and spokesperson for Halftee Layering Fashion, a business that is currently the 9th fastest growing company in Utah.

Since partnering with the company, Halftee Layering Fashions has achieved consistent triple-digit growth, month-over-month, due to her out-of-the-box approach. Spitfire that she is, Noelle has used her expertise to manage large accounts and help expand the company's presence nationwide. Since she joined the company, they were able to secure international distribution in Canada, and Australia for Halftee which is now slated to expand to Japan and the United Kingdom as well. Noelle's edginess continues to keep her companies on the cutting edge. While the apparel Noelle creates and manufactures is a prodigious product, it's the way she is building her business that adorns her empire. She has created a SOULution-based clothing line that dresses women's bodies, but more importantly embodies what women are truly about at the heart level. With the success of her businesses, she has become a television personality.

Responsible for all on air appearances as well as fashion shoots for the company, she has also been a guest host for a lifestyle television show in her state. Halftee appearances have included SHOPHQ, formally SHOPNBC, The Shopping Channel and HSN, QVC Italy, and QVC Germany. Enjoying herself during her television appearance proved suitable to encourage viewers to purchase product quickly, selling out the line in 30 seconds. This platform affords her the ability to make her viewers happy, laugh and enjoy life more. Noelle has found that the more you share your gifts, the more gifts will be shared with you. By serving her audience, her life's purpose has been served more.

Throughout Noelle's life, while she has been extremely blessed, some of her challenges have created the lane changes that have defined who she is and what defines as her purpose. She fully understands that when your world is falling apart, you have to pull it together. In dark times, she picks herself up and keeps driving ahead. As a self-motivated, driven, successful entrepreneur who has faced challenges throughout her life, Noelle always overcomes them with panache. The power in a brand is illustrated by the vision of its founder, drawn from her biggest accomplishments and her greatest tribulations. You must first make a difference before you can make money. "Nobody dictates how much I'm worth," Noelle proclaims.

The person behind the brand brings to the forefront the ability to inspire and motivate others to greatness. Always yearning to embrace the next opportunity to share her experience, Noelle enjoys serving as a spokesperson, consultant, business coach, and oftentimes a sounding board for brands or individuals passionate about taking their ideas to the next level. She provides an authentic and personal approach to business beginning with the conception of an idea and continuing all the way through to the execution of the final product. She has proven that you can create success while remaining raw and relevant.

Noelle's road to success continues to be paved by ambition. She is the living embodiment of a true renaissance woman. She has a modern fashion sense that clicks with the average consumer, a savvy business acumen that allows her to manage large accounts effortlessly, and a magnetic personality that electrifies and inspires others to take action. When dynamic individuals, like Noelle, achieve heightened success, they look around with an intense desire to reach out their hands in an effort to mentor and guide others who are equally as determined. Noelle's electric personality inspires and motivates others to take steps towards realizing overwhelming success, as well.

Noelle continues to add so much value to the world because of who she is, how much she cares about others and the unwavering commitment to fulfill her purpose and passion. When you want to get into the fast lane, shift based on what you want and what you love. There is no such thing as autopilot because life is about correcting course along the journey to allow your purpose to become your power.

You must choose to cruise and use your strengths to succeed. Whether the next challenge and opportunity is a new business venture, a new spokesperson opportunity, or something completely different, Noelle is ready to handle it with the same savvy and talent with which she handles every other aspect of her life. On the road to success, the finish line may not be the ultimate destination - the journey along the way is what life is all about. The more driven you are to accomplish your purpose and propel your vision, the more others can draft off your forward momentum.

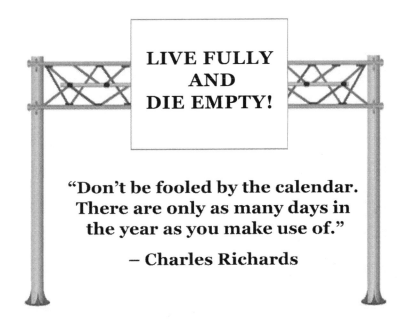

LIVE FULLY
AND
DIE EMPTY!

"Don't be fooled by the calendar.
There are only as many days in
the year as you make use of."

— Charles Richards

# Rodney Franks

Throughout life we can point to significant influencers who have accomplished so much that their accolades become farfetched; Rodney Franks is one of those individuals and yet if we could condense his commendations into one tribute, it would be the size his heart. Growing up as one of eight children in a single family, poor home, movies became an escape for Rodney which allowed him to fantasize about a different life than his less-than-perfect reality.

One of the most profound movies that had an impact on his life was "Ferris Bueller's Day Off" because it depicted the life of a young man whose life was the complete opposite of Rodney's. The premise of the movie is that Ferris skips school and steals his best friend Cameron father's red 1961 Ferrari 250GT to impress his girlfriend. As they are touring Chicago, Ferris and his friends decide to valet the car while they explored the city. Unbeknownst to Ferris, the valet drivers take the car out for a joy ride.

When Ferris and his friends finally return the car to Cameron's father's garage, astonished and fearful, they discover the high mileage on the odometer. Making their best effort to cover their tracks, they make a desperate, unsuccessful attempt to turn back the mileage.

During the overwhelming experience and the fear of wrath Cameron expects from his father, he has a commanding monologue in which he reflects on the truth that he didn't want to live his life in fear nor remain under the restraints of his father any longer. And no matter what the high mileage conveyed to his father, Cameron began to realize despite his futile efforts to alter the mileage, he cannot change the past. From his acceptance of what he has done and the impending response from his father, Cameron began to take control of his life and actions and ultimately through a short and forceful bout of regaining his power, he kicks the car and it rolls backwards out of the glass garage and down into a ravine.

The inspirational concept of being true to yourself and taking back the power of your life illustrated in his favorite movie. Rodney didn't want to turn back the mileage in his own life any longer and wish it were filled with another set of circumstances. He wanted to start living in the present and start owning his life, both the good and bad, and refusing to love with one foot on the pedal and one foot on the brake driving it in reverse.

This became Rodney's first poignant Lane Change. We all have a desire to reshape the negative experiences in our lives. While there are moments where we want to turn back the hands of time and change these experiences, it is actually those significant experiences that truly shape us. Instead of wanting to alter our past, it's our ability to embrace them and turn them into catalysts to move us forward that matters. From that point when he recognized the power of living in the present and his ability to change his own future, Rodney got into the right lane and focused on the path in front of him rather than the road behind him. Grabbing the steering wheel of his life and setting his own trajectory, he created a new path for himself. Rodney became the first person in his entire family to graduate college and he even went on to attend graduate school at St. Louis University School of Law.

"Life couldn't get any better than it was," Rodney recalls. Yet, throughout life, with every high there are lows. His family's health history was poor; his grandmother had died at the early age of 44 from a heart attack, his grandfather at 56 from the same affliction, and his brother as well at the age of 50. Rodney's mother had some health complications throughout her life but with her everlasting strength and her strong faith in God, she always pulled through. She was his best friend and greatest ambassador, unconditionally loving him throughout her entire life. They were inseparable.

During his first year of law school, visiting home because his sister was in town, Rodney's mother asked him stay the night. She asked him to watch that evening her favorite video, Bill Cosby's stand up. His mother insisted that he spend the night and enjoy more family time. Due to a prior commitment with his law buddies, Rodney decided to go to an event with them and network. As he was leaving, his mother embraced him a little longer than normal, pulling him in close and gave a big smile to him as he left. Early that next morning, Rodney received a call from his sister indicating that his mother wasn't breathing. As he sped over to his mother's house, he discovered her laying on her bedroom floor surrounded by the paramedics lifeless, she had died in her sleep from a heart attack.

Guilt of not being there when she died that night consumed Rodney and he dropped out of law school to spend time reflecting on what he truly wanted from life and sojourned to find its meaning. With every low we can use it as a navigational point of where are at the moment and it provides fuel to thrust us forward toward the high road to greatness. Nine months after his mother's death, Rodney happened to watch a rerun of "Ferris Bueller's Day Off". A gross reminder to him that he could not turn back the hands of time and to continue doing so proves to be a cumbersome impossibility. Rodney learned that his mother's life and death shaped who he was and who he will always be. It's essential that we savor every moment. "We spend so much time wanting to go back in the past that we don't truly appreciate the time we have now," he confesses.

Remembering his mother embracing him tightly her final night, he committed to squeeze every moment out of every minute of life because of the indelible impression she had left with him was just not made on Rodney, but on the countless people in her community that were blessed because of her presence. After quite a bit of soul searching, recognizing law school was not his true passion, he dedicated his life to perpetuating her dream and her commitment to the community. As a preacher, she inspired her followers that they could live a better life, and that there is a brighter day.

Throughout the reflective process, Rodney admits that his desire to become a lawyer was merely to be able to get his family out of poverty and afford them a more abundant life. While there isn't anything inherently wrong with that and it is actually completely meritorious, he was pursuing a path based on his perception of other's expectations of him. When his mother, a single parent passed away, Rodney had no one else to impress but he also had no support to fall back on. It became the perfect storm to pursue his true calling and discover that the more you give, the more you receive. In order to take care of himself, he started to give of himself.

His mother's death became the catalyst to Rodney truly living. This led him to truly follow what he wanted and what would impact others, living his life to the fullest. "You may be here today and gone tomorrow, but what are you doing in the meantime? Whose life are you inspiring? What impact are you having for people you do know and for many that you will never meet?" Rodney preaches. Rodney not only changed his path but the road for so many others by dedicating his gifts to raising over $250 million for universities, biomedical research institutes and art galleries with the inspiration from his mother's life and her unwavering dedication to revitalizing their community.

Walking through the buildings that have been built because of the funds he has raised, and seeing the faces of the many individuals who are positively affected by his philanthropic efforts, Rodney continues to pursue his passion because of the direct and indirect impact on those who have been blessed by him. He was able to capture the attention from others because of his personal story. More importantly, he was able to capture his gifts and talents and package them together, becoming a significant person of influence in the non-profit world as the youngest CEO of a foundation in the country. He implemented those aptitudes into a strategy that has significant impact on institutions across the country.

Perhaps each of us, by truly living intentional lives of purpose and passion, can inspire others by our own example of living life to its fullest. As words don't teach, our giving of ourselves to others is the greatest demonstration of a lane change we can ever make. The best way to help others is to live our best lives. Rodney believes that the ability to create the greatest affect in the world is at the intersection of your passion and your service to others.

Driving forward, while his life has been focused on living in the present, there comes a time in each person's life where they look back and see how much life they've lived and look forward and see how much they still have to live. In either glance, having such an appreciation of the culmination of all the events in your life – both good and bad- will shape your charity, your joy, your patience, your love, your strategy and your success. Focusing on his gifts of motivation and inspiration, he volunteers on boards in order to create a greater reach of influence and impact and he spreads his experience to individuals and to thousands.

What drives Rodney is improving the lives of others, in a small or grandiose way. Acknowledging that creating success is often at the cost of many trials and tribulations, Rodney continues to remain grateful for the many blessings that afforded him the opportunity to utilize his gifts. Raised as a preacher's son, he was able to hear many sermons and also gave him the chance to speak at a young age. The first time he spoke at 9 years old in front of his mother's congregation, it was dead silent in the church. Worried he had done something unholy, he discovered later that the worshipers were quiet because they were so moved by his immense talent. They were witnessing a young boy utilizing his God-given gifts while Rodney was discovering them first-hand. The experience of moving people emotionally as a result of sharing his personal story, along with his exquisite skills of influencing and creating powerful impressions, combined, make it possible for him to express into power what wasn't even possible. Rodney's true gift of public speaking would become a present to everyone who had the fortune to hear him.

Established now as a prominent influencer, Rodney believes that to get into the fast lane you must combine your natural abilities with massive practice and consistent rehearsal. You can have the greatest vehicle in the world, but a smooth road doesn't make a skilled driver. Rodney has become one of the most sought after orators. His proven track record of monumental, tangible results catapulted him into the top tier of motivational speakers. Entrepreneurship is challenging, yet when you get into the right lane suited just for you there is not traffic. You become willing to continue driving the world forward because of your desire to help others get on their road to success. Over his personal journey of letting go of what he didn't want and accepting what he truly wanted, Rodney used the wisdom he gained over his career to incorporate into his new venture as a leading transformational keynote speaker.

Rodney acknowledges his wealth is not in the things he can create in a business, but rather built in what he can create in a relationship. When you have challenges in your business or faced with the most devastating moment of your life, you change your relationship with money and focus on savoring relationships with people. When you are at a crossroads, you turn to those who will support you. People are Rodney's greatest currency. For those who are blessed enough to have a relationship with him, the greatest return on their investment is spending time with one of the most amazing humans the world has ever known.

Rodney's life and career have been marked by wildly impressive milestones and his journey on the road to success via the entrepreneurial highway has been signified by mile markers that paved the road to success for so many. Shifting gears, he has transitioned from working for other companies creating extraordinary results to becoming the driver of his own destiny. Launching his consulting business, he is able to exercise his talents and gifts fully to serve others.

The philosophy Rodney has incorporated into his life and business for his own success, in order to create triumph for others, is getting AMPED:

Assess

Map out a

Plan

Execute

Deliver

Despite the unknown, Rodney founded RDF Consulting because of his passion for entrepreneurship and independency. He has discovered the more action he takes the less fearful he becomes. You can listen to words of doubt or you can drown out the noise of fear and breakthrough your limiting beliefs by believing that anything is possible when you get AMPED.

Beautifully, by pursuing his passions and getting into the correct lane for him, he has been able to become more financially successful, more confident in his skills and he has created more time to fully live out his dreams. The quality of his life has surpassed his expectations. Rodney continues to live fully so he can die empty. "If God has given me all these gifts, talents and opportunities, my job is to meet Him where He is. I want to make sure my talents are fully given to this world, that my dreams are fully realized, that there will never be a 'should of, could of, would of,'" Rodney confesses. When you believe in yourself, coupled with your faith in God, and you follow a plan, you can live an abundant, significant life.

On the road to our greatest life, the destination we are seeking is only achieved by maximizing our capacity to give and contribute. The best way to do that is to follow the lane that will lead you to your greatest potential. Other drivers in your life will want to instruct you on how to be happy, yet you hold the wheel that will direct your ultimate destiny. Rodney's ability to influence others is impeccable. The results of this skill are because of his ability to influence his own life. The journey of life is an epic expedition of self-actualization and results-driven strategic growth. "It's been so fun getting out of the slow lane and into the fast lane. I'm not pumping the breaks. It's pedal to the medal and it's been a great ride so far," Rodney boldly proclaims!

Find the right direction for your life. Go the right speed for you. If you're unhappy with either, make a Lane Change. Rodney reflectively professes that a powerful way to discover your lane is to discover your purpose and he further explains that its discovery lies in your prayer and meditation. He defines praying as communicating to God and meditating is listening from God. You have been given gifts that only you can bring to the world. You have been equipped with the abilities to transform the world in ways only specifically designed for you. The landscape of the world can be changed by your willingness to make the transition, step up and step out into your truth.

The Fast Lane was designed for a purpose. If you want to go fast, go alone. If you want to go far, go together. Rodney is creating a movement and a legacy by helping people go faster and further than they ever thought possible. The extra mile is often empty because people aren't willing to get there. With Rodney's service, they are getting there. Through his passion for others, he is empowering individuals and organizations to live a fulfilled life and a passionate purpose. Those whose lives are overflowing, avidly live their greatest life by fueling it with their talents, missional focus and a passion to change the world. Getting into the fast lane with Rodney is one of those reasons. Are you ready to take the wheel?

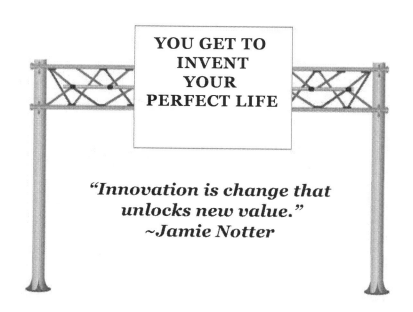

"Innovation is change that
unlocks new value."
~Jamie Notter

# Ron Klein

Ron Klein has a zest for life and a magnetic energy that fills the hearts of every person who has the privilege and opportunity to be around him. And for those who won't ever meet Ron in person, he has had an impact on your life and you carry a little piece of his genius everywhere you go, every day! That's right! Among numerous everyday inventions we utilize, Ron is the innovative originator of the magnetic strips on our debit and credit cards.

You will find that at 80 years old his brain and his body move faster than most people a quarter his age. He has changed the landscape of our business world through his inventions. More importantly, he has changed the landscape of our society by touching hearts and impacting lives of millions, because of the person he is and the passion he has for teaching others. "Money is the easiest thing to make. You've got to make people happy," Ron exclaims as he reflects on the fact that as an opportunist he never truly had a strategic plan in his entire life.

Ron tends to recognize an opportunity when it smacks him right in the face. While he doesn't see the big picture right away, the opportunities manifest themselves and send Ron in a new direction that he can use to solve a problem. He essentially allows possibilities to direct him and he creates lane changes intentionally to turn a possibility into an opportunity! From a working class family, after serving in the military, Ron used his GI bill to get an engineering degree. Early on, he was intrigued not just about the operational components and how they worked, but why they worked inside and out. He became an investigator. He read a lot, asked a lot of questions and paid attention – pay attention in life and you'll eventually get paid a lot.

While Ron was first-class is his technical abilities, he also studied marketing and sales. He was able to become a bridge that could connect the clients on the technical side to the development and create a new world of effectiveness. Ron became a professional problem solver. He had an uncanny ability to recognize the 'givens' and then create a solution, typically to speed up a process. While Ron was working for a big company he wanted to make more money, but the company wasn't able to pay him. This lane change actually helped him turn the challenge into an opportunity. He quit and went into business for himself.

When you provide value, people and opportunities seek you. He obtained clients because they knew he was an asset and because of his ability to see a possibility and find the solution. The more projects Ron got, the bigger his company grew.

Ron always had the ability to create a desire and when he didn't know what he needed to completely solve the problem he would study and research. To produce the results he wanted, he needed more money. To get more money, he simply added more value and went on a mission to learn what he needed to obtain what he didn't have. Often times we become limited by our resource when all we need to do is become more resourceful. As his company grew, so did his problems. And with increased problems came increased possibilities. Ron never looked at challenges as obstacles, but rather as the ability to create a lane change.

He has guts and with his ferocious fortitude for productivity, acquiring the nickname "The smiling cobra," his leadership continually turns those who don't see his vision into his biggest advocates. His consistent ability to triumph through tribulation earned him genuine and loyal followers who pushed his vision forward to create massive success for all around him. Ron found himself with the ability financially to retire at 34. And he did for 60 days until he realized that his passion was more important. Yet, with the credibility he had created he was able to design his ideal lifestyle around his work rather than having to work to create a lifestyle. You can't argue with success.

Throughout the next few years as his reputation attracted more clients, he did everything from creating program trading and the bond trading system on the New York Stock Exchange to creating the Multiple Listing Service for realtors and even created a formula to grow chickens to full maturity in 8 weeks for Frank Purdue. With the massive success, specifically from automating the New York Stock Exchange Ron went into retirement again around age 60. Yet, his desire to help others solve problems was far too great. Throughout his life the only thing that Ron has failed at is retirement. You can't keep a good man down and his passion to create is too powerful. Even to this day when Ron is approached to help find a solution to a problem he says yes, and then figures it out. Often in life we feel we need all the answers before taking action. Often it pays to take action and make shifts along the way to create the results.

Ron has focused his life helping people who need it. He did it with a selfless desire to solve problems. He never had a strategic plan, but he was always a strategic thinker. The results he has created in his life are often unfathomable and yet because of the person he is and the heart-centered mission he has for creating lane changes, he has taken his life and the lives of so many directly and indirectly into the fast lane. Throughout the course of his career inventing some of the most obvious solutions (at least to him), Ron discovered his philosophy to take your life into overdrive. To become the driver of your entrepreneurial life you need to be:

→ Smart – pay attention to what's around you and what's going on.

→ Daring – Don't be afraid to make mistakes because the mistake can teach you a lesson and you'll be able to get out of a problem, even if it's one you created.

→ Different – Sell benefits, not ideas.

Your reality will become fulfilled in relation to your adaptability. The reality is that all roads are connected and lead to another road. Your ability to follow one and be open to the opportunity to take another one will determine your reality. The lane that is best for you may be determined by the need to travel down it. Sometimes we need a destination to start the journey and sometimes we just need to start the journey and adjust the wheel in the direction that will take us to our ideal life.

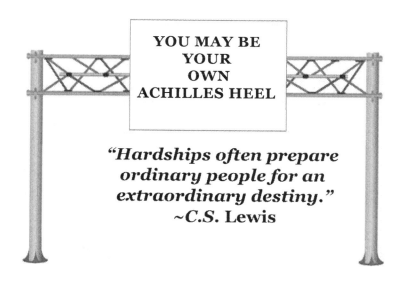

"*Hardships often prepare ordinary people for an extraordinary destiny.*"
~C.S. Lewis

# Terri Levine

Time is like a river because you cannot touch the same water twice since the flow that has passed will never pass again. And throughout life we can never re-live the same moment, but those moments can create a new direction that truly allows our lives to flow. Terri Levine learned through the people in her life that the most precious time we can spend is with the ones we love, doing what we love. Terri was extremely focused on her work and was accomplished in society's version of success. Yet, as her mother was slowly dying from emphysema, Terri realized that her priorities were messed up. At the same time, her best friend, who was in a hospice, was dying from breast cancer.

Talking on the phone to her friend, who also put work as a top priority in life, Terri heard something for the first time that would disrupt the value she put on work and redirect it to putting value on things that truly mattered. "Life is not about work and it's not about people standing up at your funeral and talking about all the things that you've done," Terri's friend reminded her.

With the passing of her mother and seven days later her best friend, Terri was challenged. While attending her best friend's funeral, listening to people stand and profess all the things that her friend had accomplished, Terri broke into tears. The thing that her friend didn't want at her funeral was happening. Terri realized that your "To Do's" are never truly done until you are truly done with your time on Earth. As the President of a national health care company at the time, Terri lived her life by her daily planner. After that week of funerals, she threw it in the trash. She went from focusing on doing, to being and living. She began focusing on her top three priorities for each day, which may have been as simple as laughing, being fully present and spending quality time with her husband.

Making a great living wasn't joyful anymore and she lost passion for her work. She started to realize what made her truly happy. She began attending personal development events. She went from being a people pleaser to having pleasure being present with them. She began determining what in her work and her life would please her. She created a lifestyle out of doing what she loved and farming out the aspects of her work that she didn't enjoy. She also hired a life coach to support her in truly creating a lifestyle marked by pleasure and joy rather than a life marked by accomplishing things.

Getting a life coach was one of the biggest lane changes for Terri because it opened her mind to the possibility that she could design a life around coaching others the way she was being coached. She began carrying around a resignation letter for three months. But she couldn't resign. She went back and forth between the fear of holding on to what she had, and the fear of letting go. Sitting at her office one day, looking at a painting of her mother with a heavy grief still on her heart, she asked her mother in the painting, "Do you want me to miserable at

work or would you like me to be happy in my life?"
Through the tears streaming down her face, knowing the
answer to that question, she resigned from her job.

Too often in life we allow the reality we know to
limit us from the reality we want to create. One of the most
freeing things we can do in life is resign from the aspects of
our lives that don't bring joy, happiness and fulfillment to
it. Perhaps this is your time to resign from those things in
your life – grief, anger, scarcity, self-worth, resentment,
limiting beliefs, a relationship, your job – that hold you
back in order to begin a new life designed your way. The
day Terri resigned is the day she started her new business.
She had 30 coaching clients in the first 30 days. "I've never
looked back. I'm loving what I do and doing what I love.
Finally, I'm at home doing what I'm meant to do making a
difference in the world. I'm affecting people, I'm impacting
people and I'm actually doing something where I'm of
service to people." Terri was in the driver's seat of her on
life.

At least until she hit a speed bump that nearly
forced her off the road. Driving in her convertible to meet
her personal trainer, she was giving gratitude for all she
had in her life and how fortunate she was to have the
vehicle of coaching to provide her a life she so greatly
appreciated. As she was working out, she heard a sound
that almost mirrored that of a gunshot. As a black belt in
jiu jitsu and someone who raced performance vehicles,
Terri knew her body well. As she put her foot down she
realized she had torn her Achilles tendon. When she was at
the hospital, she went into shock and after months of
excruciating pain, they discovered that she had developed
reflex sympathetic dystrophy, a rare degenerative disease
of which there is no cure.

This set up a challenge in her personal life and her
ability to perform but also her professional life and her

ability to coach, sometimes screaming in agonizing pain for 6 hours a day. One day, the pain was so excruciating and she was so frustrated that she sat at her computer to write her goodbye letter. She was ready to end it all. Hours passed and what started out as a death letter became a book called "Magnetize" that has actually helped others truly live. Researching RSD, Terri realized that this disease was the most common disease to lead people to commit suicide. She also realized that millions of children were struggling with the same complications she experienced. Terri started a foundation for children with RSD and has become a voice and an advocate for children who need care.

Straight roads do not make skillful drivers. Through running into her biggest challenge, she realized that she could create a massive change from her bump in the road. Fear often becomes our own Achilles heel in running our true race in life. The key is not to let the things that hold us back cripple us from moving forward, one step at a time. Terri believes there are four steps we can each take toward a better life: The first step is to focus on what you desire, rather than what you don't want. Then ignite a fire within yourself because change doesn't happen until you become really passionate about what you want in life. The next step would be to create a technicolor vision of those things to the point where you can taste, smell and feel them.

The next step is to take a physical action. Finally, create an intentional gratitude practice into your daily routine. Like the wheels on a car, we need all four of these to be able to drive forward. During our journeys, through the trials and tribulations that we face, we must utilize them to help drive the world forward. Often times in our need to always be the best, we prohibit ourselves from learning from people who have lessons we need to learn. There is a balance between being righteous and always being right. Often our ego is not our amigo. The people who enter our lives and the experiences we encounter allow us to truly discover the fuel the drives us. Terri has transitioned from valuing materialistic things to materializing things for her non-profit. The lane that Terri is driving down is paved with openness and an understanding that the biggest blessings in the world may come from the biggest detours in our lives. She has made a dramatic shift from being an entrepreneur to what she has trademarked as a Heartrepreneur – someone who leads and aids selflessly for others. "Life is a journey. Every detour that we have makes us who we are. Every single one of us is totally perfect with all of our imperfections. Being who we are and sharing who we are is what helps people learn. Sharing our mistakes is what helps others go forward and not make those same mistakes and have an easier road."

While her mother passed from a complication and a struggle to breathe, Terri is using her life to breathe hope into others at a heart level. Our success is not predicated on our ability to do and perform but rather on our ability to love and to serve. We will all certainly face our own complication to breathe at certain times in life. It may not be shortness of breath but it will be shortness of vision for our lives, shortness of gratitude for everything in our lives, shortness of the will to continue when the risk seems far greater than the reward and shortness of the necessary commitment to making a lane change and keep driving forward. This is your time to take that next step. This is your time to make a shift. This is your time to accelerate your dreams.

**CONTRIBUTING AUTHORS**

A special acknowledgment and token of gratitude to all of the contributing experts for pouring their hearts and souls into this project. Without you, it wouldn't have been possible. With you, anything is possible. Your selfless commitment to "Life in the Fast Lane" serves as an illustration of how you live your lives every day. Your stories will impact so many people through this collaborative effort. We are eternally grateful to you. YOU are the reason it will be an extremely impactful book. Together, we are creating a REVolution of Lane Changers who are living "Life in the Fast Lane."

# Betsy Allen-Manning

Featured on FOX, CBS, ABC & NBC, Betsy is known for helping leaders and their staff get motivated to achieve higher levels of success, and even wrote the audio book on it-The TRIUMPH Method. She's also a co-author of The People Advantage.

With 15 + years' experience as a leader for multi-billion dollar corporations, Betsy has developed training programs for the Golden Globe events and Steve Wynn's $70-million-dollar establishment-EBC. Some of her top clients include: Toshiba, BMW, and The U.S. Dept. of Defense; where her focus is turning paycheck employees into effective leaders.

As one of the top motivational speakers on leadership & organizational development, Betsy travels nationwide, helping managers gain credibility, respect and become more effective as a leader.

www.BetsyAllenManning.com
betsy@betsyallenmanning.com


# Brenda Geary

Brenda Geary is a corporate executive turned entrepreneur and motivational speaker. After 2 decades as a successful human resources executive in a Fortune 50 Company, her world was turned upside down when she developed a number of auto immune diseases including cancer. As a result of overcoming her health challenges, Brenda is now passionate about sharing her story of recovery and educating and inspiring others on how to achieve and maintain optimal wellness. Brenda lives in San Diego, CA and is married to the love of her life Randy.

You can connect with Brenda at [brenda@brendageary.com](mailto:brenda@brendageary.com)

## Craig Duswalt

Craig Duswalt is a Speaker, Author, Podcast Host, YouTube Personality and the creator of *RockStar Marketing*.

Craig's background includes touring with Guns N' Roses, as Axl Rose's personal assistant, and Air Supply, as the band's personal assistant.

Craig was also an award-winning copywriter, working as a Creative Director for a Los Angeles-based ad agency until opening up his own ad agency, Green Room Design & Advertising, which was named the 2002 Santa Clarita Valley Chamber of Commerce Small Business of the Year.

Craig combined his backgrounds in both music and marketing and now promotes his *RockStar Events* all over the country, where he teaches entrepreneurs, small businesses, home-based businesses and the self-employed how to promote themselves and their business by thinking outside the box. Craig's signature event is his 2 1/2-Day *RockStar Marketing BootCamp* every March and September in Los Angeles.

Craig Duswalt also speaks to corporations on how to market like a RockStar, to colleges about drug awareness, and at numerous seminars, associations and conferences, teaching entrepreneurs how to use outside the box marketing techniques to attract clients, and how to stand out from the competition — *Like a RockStar*.

Craig will be speaking across the country on his new *Rock Your Life* World Tour in 2017.

## Daniel Moirao

Dr. Dan motivates, trains and coaches' leaders in developing productive and profitable cultures where everyone is motived for success. Dr. Dan guides leaders to identify their leadership style, the style that dominates the culture and how that intersection of those can increase productivity and profitability.

Dr. Dan has been recognized as a "pioneer in reform" as well as a "distinguished educator". He works extensively with leadership teams in recognizing the internal and external culture and how to use that culture to leverage change for sustainability.   Through his work with leaders he has developed leaders focused on creating a "thoughtful" climate, a "thoughtful" culture, and "thoughtful" cooperation.

Dr. Dan has served a Superintendent of schools in vastly diverse multicultural communities. He is a certified executive coach; and trainer of leadership styles, strategic planner and facilitator. Dr. Moirao is a dynamic leader, trainer, teacher, and keynote speaker for administrators, teachers, and parents.

## Dottie Kelley

Dottie Kelley, the "Entrepreneurial Gypsy," has a passion for change and thrives in creating new business opportunities.

By the time she was 24 years old she had already owned and sold two successful small businesses, fulfilled one of her life long dreams to becoming an actress, was the co-founder of a non-profit and took her life-changing journey on *in-line skates*, from Canada to Mexico.

Dottie is also a licensed Real Estate Agent.

Contact Dottie on Facebook @EntreGypsy.com


## Elliot Grossbard

Elliot Grossbard is the founder of Disruptive Sales Consulting. Disruptive Sales helps companies disrupt stagnant sales, clarify their brand, and improve culture and correct ineffective marketing by collecting the right targeted customer's attention.

Disruptive Sales was developed and molded through Elliot's sales experience which includes the roll out in Florida of the largest computer training company when Windows 95 launched in the 90's, partnered in the management of a portfolio in excess of $400 million in assets during the height of the technology bubble and the aftermath, building a sales force for a national company that provides educational and commercial furniture, and his own company SupplyMart—an office supply company that focuses on small and mid-size companies with customers across the U.S.


Through 20+ years in sales – Elliot has established core values that have been shared with his sales teams, companies, and clients; as a result of implementing Disruptive Sales into their own organization, often they experience increased sales, brand expansion, happier and more dedicated employees, and a new and passionate culture.

The largest reward for any salesperson, whether an account executive or CEO of a Fortune 500 company, is: "When you deliver on a promise, execute a service, or simply give your customer a solution – that satisfaction alone is what should be the inner drive of every true salesperson."

Elliot is passionate about the things he loves, and that starts with his family down to his loyalty to his hometown Detroit Red Wings, Tigers, and Lions sports teams. Living in Miami for 25 years where he fell in love with the Miami Heat in the 90s, he has aligned himself with essential people in the South Florida business community that has enabled him to be a resource (POI) for people in his network. His family consists of his wife of 21 years, and 3 children.

Email: elliot@disruptivesalesconsulting.com
Phone: (305) 306-**SELL** (7355)

LinkedIn Profile And Articles:
www.linkedin.com/in/elliotgrossbard/

Twitter: @ElliotOneT @salesdisrupter
Facebook: www.facebook.com/egrossbard

Instagram: @elliot.one.t @disruptivesales
Snapchat: ElliotOneT

## Frank Shankwitz

Frank Shankwitz is best known as the creator and a founder of the Make-A-Wish Foundation, an extraordinary charity that grants the wishes to children with life-threating illnesses. From humble beginnings, the Make-A-Wish Foundation is now a global organization that grants a child's wish somewhere in the world on an average of every 28 minutes. Frank is a U.S. Air Force veteran, and has a long and distinguished career in law enforcement. He began as an Arizona Highway Patrol Motorcycle Officer, and retired as a Homicide Detective with the Arizona Department of Public Safety, with 42 years of service. Frank has been featured in numerous publications and television programs, and has received several awards, including the White House Call to Service Award from President George W. Bush.

In 2015 Frank joined six U.S. Presidents as well as Nobel Prize winners and industry leaders as a recipient of the Ellis Island Medal of Honor. In December, 2015, Frank was presented with an Honorary Doctorate Degree, Doctor of Public Service, from The Ohio State University. In December, 2015, Frank was identified as one of the "10 Most Amazing Arizonans" in a front page article in the Arizona Republic newspaper. In January, 2016, Frank was identified in a Forbes Magazine article as a Top Ten Keynote Speaker. Frank's new book, "Wishman" was released in October, 2016 and is available at Amazon.com. Frank's life story will soon be featured in an upcoming motion picture, "Wish Man".

Further information is available on Frank's website, wishman1.com.


## Gina Ruby

Gina Ruby is a Certified Health Coach, Life Strategist, and Passionista for life!! Her 15 years of acting and modeling along with her 11 years of health and wellness have equipped her to share the message that everyone can create a healthier version of themselves both physically and mentally if they want it. She's living proof that it can be done since she had to start from scratch at the age of 40. Going from victim to victor IS possible!

When she's not speaking, writing, or networking, you can find Gina singing in her church's band, riding her motorcycle, or finding the next fun mountain to climb! She is madly in love with her Lord Jesus and her husband Andy and she is blessed to have an amazing bonus daughter. Gina's motto through thick and thin is: "Joy is a choice, choose it!"

You can connect with Gina at ginaruby1@gmail.com and www.PursueHealth.TSFL.com

## Greg Writer

Greg Writer is a C level executive with over thirty years' experience in corporate finance, capital formation, executive level management, mergers, acquisitions, software development and sales/marketing.

Greg became the youngest owner of a full service investment bank in the history of United States. During this period Greg helped raise millions for early stage companies like: Home Shopping Network, Smarte Carts, Go Video Dual Deck VCR.

In an effort to perpetuate free enterprise & capitalism he launched Angel Investors Network in 1997 with the mission to "help entrepreneurs succeed."

He is very passionate about the formation of earlier stage companies and believes this is crucial to the economy of the United States. He wrote the book *"Saving America One Crowd @ A Time"*, which was one of the 1st books to be written around the new Crowdfunding Laws.

Greg has coached thousands of entrepreneurs marketing strategies and has been teaching on stages across the United States since 2004.

He is currently CEO of Angel Investors Network, Angel Marketing, Inspiration By God, BizPAD and President of Celebrity Lifestyle Brands. He serves on the Board of Never Give Up, a non-profit.

Greg is the proud father of 5 and has been married for 30 years.

You can connect more www.AngelNetwork.com or www.gregwriter.com

# Haris Reis

Haris Reis is the President of Changing Lanes International. He is also a National Award Winning Entrepreneur, #1 National Best-Selling Author, Keynote Speaker and Elite Marketing Consultant.

He has helped Changing Lanes International become a 6-figure business in a year. He was previously a growth hacker at VaynerMedia building Gary Vaynerchuk's personal brand and ran paid media for the top 1% users on Facebook. The videos he has created have been shared with people that have over 130k followers, has been in videos that collectively reached over 1.5 million people, created videos that cumulatively received over 4.4 million views, and has produced nearly $100k in sales for products/services over the phone.

He has been featured in The Young Entrepreneurs podcast, College Startup, Collegiate Entrepreneurs' Organization, Live Out Loud, Experts Showcase, The Ambitious Life Magazine and the Life Leveraging Series.

Haris is a very proud immigrant from Bosnia and is a 22-year old college student.

You can connect with Haris at harisreis@gmail.com or follow him on:
Snapchat - bosnianbean
Instagram - Haris.reis
Facebook - Haris.reis

## Jeff Hoffman

Jeff Hoffman is a successful entrepreneur, proven CEO, worldwide motivational speaker, Hollywood film producer, and a producer of a Grammy-winning jazz album in 2015. In his career, he has been the founder of multiple startups, he has been the CEO of both public and private companies, and he has served as a senior executive in many capacities. Jeff has been part of a number of well-known companies, including Priceline.com. uBid.com, CTI, ColorJar, and more.

Jeff serves on boards of companies in the US, Europe, South America, Africa, and Asia, supporting entrepreneurs and small businesses in more than 150 countries. He supports the White House, the US State Department, the United Nations, and many foreign governments on economic growth initiatives and entrepreneurship programs.

Jeff is a frequent keynote speaker, having been invited to speak in over 50 countries. He speaks on the topics of innovation, entrepreneurship, and business leadership, and is the co-author of the book SCALE, a how-to guide for growing your business. Jeff also teaches innovation workshops to major corporations on a regular basis.

Jeff is a featured business expert seen on Fox News, Fox Business, CNN, CNN International, Bloomberg News, CNBC, ABC, and NPR, and in publications including Forbes, Inc., Time, Fast Company, the Wall Street Journal, and more.

Outside of the world of technology, Jeff has produced movies, has produced musical events including concerts, tours, and charity events with such artists as Elton John, Britney Spears, NSYNC, and others, and serves on numerous charity and non-profit boards.

You can email him jeff@colorjar.com or connect at www.jeffhoffman.com

# Jeff Garcia

Jeffrey Garcia is a former American football and Canadian football quarterback. After attending high school and junior college in Gilroy, California, Garcia played college football at San Jose State University.

A four-time CFL All-Star and four-time NFL Pro Bowl selection, Garcia began his professional football career with the Calgary Stampeders of the Canadian Football League (CFL) as an undrafted free agent in 1994. In 1999, Garcia debuted in the National Football League (NFL) with the San Francisco 49ers. With the 49ers, Garcia made three Pro Bowl appearances (for the 2000, 2001, and 2002 seasons) and led the team to the playoffs in the 2001 and 2002 seasons. With the Philadelphia Eagles, Garcia would return to form late in the 2006 season, starting for an injured Donovan McNabb and leading Philadelphia to the playoffs. Garcia joined the Tampa Bay Buccaneers in 2007 and was starting quarterback for most games of the 2007 and 2008 seasons. Again, Garcia led Tampa Bay to the playoffs in 2007 and made his fourth career Pro Bowl appearance.

Garcia is one of only ten quarterbacks in NFL history who have achieved two consecutive thirty-touchdown passing seasons (2000 and 2001) at least one time in their career. The others are Philip Rivers, Steve Bartkowski, Drew Brees, Peyton Manning, Brett Favre, Dan Fouts, Dan Marino, Tom Brady, Aaron Rodgers, and Eli Manning. He is also one of only thirteen quarterbacks to throw a 99-yard touchdown pass.

## John Lee Dumas

John Lee Dumas is the host of EOFire, an award winning Podcast where he interviews today's most successful Entrepreneurs 7-days a week. JLD has interviewed over 1400 Entrepreneurs and EOFire has over 1 million monthly listens. If you're looking to accomplish your #1 goal in 100 days, John's record setting Freedom Journal is waiting for you at TheFreedomJournal.com!

## Kevin Harrington

Kevin Harrington has been a successful entrepreneur over the last 40 years. He is an Original Shark on the ABC hit, Emmy winning TV show, "Shark Tank." He is also the Inventor of the Infomercial, As Seen On TV Pioneer, Co-Founder of the Electronic Retailers Association (ERA) and

Co- Founder of the Entrepreneurs' Organization (EO). Kevin has launched over 20 businesses that have grown to over $100 million in sales each, has been involved in more than a dozen public companies, and has launched over 500 products generating more than $5 billion in sales worldwide.

Kevin got his start as a young entrepreneur in the early 80's when he invested $25,000 and launched Quantum International. This turned in to a $500 million per year business on the New York Stock Exchange and drove the stock price from $1 to $20 per share. After selling his interest in Quantum International, he formed a joint Venture with the Home Shopping Network, called HSN Direct, which grew to hundreds of millions of dollars in sales. Entrepreneur Magazine has called him one of the top Entrepreneurs of our time.

The true value of Kevin is not only the 40 years of his knowledge of building businesses but also what he can do for other companies in many industries with his global Rolodex and his ability to solve problems.

To learn more about Kevin, please visit www.KevinHarrington.tv and watch this short video here: https://www.youtube.com/watch?v=5HLthP3l2_E

## Mark Lack

Mark Lack is the host of the #1 business show in America, Business Rockstars. He is also the bestselling author of "Shorten The Gap," which is endorsed by world renowned experts in the personal development industry. Mark is an entrepreneur and millennial thought leader who coaches people to greater success through creating the life of their dreams while becoming financially free.

Connect with Mark more at:

ShortenTheGap.com

## Nik Halik

Nik Halik is the founder and CEO of Financial Freedom Institute, Lifestyle Revolution, 5 Day Weekend and The Thrillionaires. His entrepreneurial freedom lifestyle story started at age 14. Nik's group of companies have financially educated and life coached over 1 Million clients in over 57 countries. He has trekked to over 138 countries, whilst generating passive income, building recurring subscription businesses, investing in tech start ups, touring with BON JOVI with his rock band, rocketing to space as a Russian trained Astronaut, having lunch on the shipwreck Titanic, HALO skydive jumping off the summit of Mt Everest, climbing into the crater of an exploding erupting volcano [1,700 Degrees Fahrenheit] just to take a selfie and just recently, entering the hermit kingdom of North Korea to expose a sweat shop factory operating illegally for an American conglomerate. He currently resides in Los Angeles, South Beach Miami and the Greek Islands.

You can learn more at www.NikHalikLive.com

## Noelle Nieporte

Extreme challenges, whether in everyday life or business, are nothing new to Noelle Nieporte. This self-motivated, driven, entrepreneur has faced challenges throughout her life, and always overcome them with panache. This ability to rise to the occasion shows itself most obviously in her dual roles as an owner and spokesperson for Halftee, a business that is the 9th fastest growing company in the state. Noelle's path to success reveals that her gung-ho attitude and boundless determination have been a central part of her essence for decades. Early in her career, she rose to prominence when she was crowned Miss Pennsylvania 1992. Enjoying the challenges and excitement of working on the stage, she continued to appear on television, performing hosting duties on several national shopping channels, and for her Lifestyle brand, Signed Noelle. Her engaging personality and zest for life resonated with audiences, often selling out clothing lines in as little as 30 seconds. Noelle is the living embodiment of a true renaissance woman. She has a modern fashion sense that clicks with the average consumer, a savvy business acumen that allows her to manage large accounts effortlessly, and a magnetic personality that electrifies and inspires others to take action. When asked directly about her personality, Noelle describes herself as a spitfire. The description seems apt, though she clearly has a more mellow side as well. In addition to her accomplishments in the business world, she is also a loving wife and mother of three girls, taking as much pride in her entrepreneurial success as she does in raising her family. Website: www.signednoelle.com

Email: support@noellenieporte.com

IG: Signednoelle

Direct Line: 801-404-9906

## Rodney Franks

Coming from a single parent home, Rodney's mother's death at age 22, when he was in his first year of law school became the catalyst for Rodney to truly live life fully and authentically.

Rodney not only changed his path, but he also changed direction. Dedicating his talent of influencing people through powerful storytelling, he has raised over $250 million for universities, biomedical research institutes and art museums with the inspiration from his mother's life and her unwavering dedication to helping others.

Because of his passion for helping others and his ability to inspire so many, he soon became one of the youngest CEO's of a foundation in the country.

His true gift of public speaking and his pursuit of lifting the spirits of others while giving them tangible ways of improving their lives and business, makes him a sought after speaker today from universities to corporations both locally, nationally and internationally.

www.rodneyfranks.com

## Ron Klein

Ron Klein is an ordinary man who accomplishes extraordinary things. He is a PROBLEM SOLVER. Every solution has resulted in monumental change, either in a new invention or a simple solution.

His innovative ideas have changed the world. He is the inventor of the Magnetic Strip on the Credit Card, Credit Card Validity Checking System and the developer of computerized systems for Real Estate (MLS) Multiple Listing Services, Voice Response for the Banking Industry and BOND Quotation and Trade Information for the New York Stock Exchange.

Ron's latest patent is for a device that enables a visually impaired person the ability to identify an item when in physical range of that item. It utilizes a smartphone and special coded adhesive labels.

Ron is a strategic advisor - consultant - mentor - problem solver and speaker.


THE GRANDFATHER OF POSSIBILITIES TM
Leading The Way with New Innovations for The Future
*Strategic Advisor - Mentor - Entrepreneur - Inventor - Speaker*
email: ronklein@4ronklein.com
website: http://www.thegrandfatherofpossibilities.com

941-374-5739


# Terri Levine

Dr. Levine is the Chief Heart-repreneur® and Founder of the Heart-repreneur® Movement. She is the bestselling author of over seventeen books and the owner of Comprehensive Coaching U, Inc.

As a keynote speaker, Terri has inspired hundreds of thousands of people through her high-content, memorable, and motivational speeches. She has been featured in the media on platforms such as ABC, NBC, MSNBC, CNBC,

Fortune, Forbes, Shape, Self, The New York Times, the BBC, and in more than fifteen hundred publications.

Terri was named one of the top ten coaching gurus in the world by www.coachinggurus.net and the top female coach in the world. She also hosts her own radio show, The Terri Levine Show: Business Advice You Can Take to The Bank.

Holding a PhD in clinical psychology, she operates www.heartrepreneur.com, mentoring business owners to turbocharge their business to create more revenues and profits while learning to be Heartrepreneurs.

Terri is also on the advisory board of several companies and dedicates time fundraising for the nonprofit foundation she founded, The Terri Levine Foundation for Children with RSD.
(www.TerriLevinefoundationforchildrenwithRSD.org)

Changing Lanes International will help you find success when life shifts. Our mission is not to change people; it's to give them the ability to change what they need in order to change their path to absolute abundance. We want you to be a part of the Changing Lanes community so we can impact the world in a greater way. You are a Lane Changer.

Accelerate. Your. Dreams.

Ready to write your own book? Connect at
www.PaveYourOwnLane.com

Want to be a bestselling author with Changing Lanes International? Email info@ChangingLanesNOW.com today and learn how to participate in an upcoming collaboration.

You can also visit us at:
www.ChangingLanesInternational.com

Want a 90-day game plan to accelerate your dreams and get your business into the fast lane? Go to www.ChangingLanesInternational.com to get your FREE consultation!

Make a shift. Take Your Life Into Overdrive. ACCELERATE YOUR DREAMS.
Get in the Fast Lane To Financial Freedom
10 Miles To Financial Freedom in 90 Days

Put the Pedal to the Metal on Your Road to Success
#1 Amazon Bestseller
On cover of 2 Magazines
Spoken on stages with the top leaders in the personal development/leadership industry
Built business that expands in 6 countries

Feel like your stuck and want to Change Lanes?

## You need a GPS to guide you down the right road.

We will help you take your life into overdrive and accelerate your dreams
in 90 days on the path to financial freedom.

## A Proven Step by Step Fast Lane Formula to Reach your Financial Destination while avoiding the common detours.

# Previous Books from Changing Lanes International

# MEET THE CHANGING LANES TEAM

Lane Ethridge is the Founder & CEO of Changing Lanes International. He is a phenomenal visionary as a creative marketing and speaker trainer. He built a business around empowering entrepreneurs to maximize their gifts and skills to drive their business forward. He is a communication master and helps you craft your message to create millions. Engaging people is about their needs, not ours.

 Changing Lanes International helps entrepreneurs increase their Recognition (Visibility), AUTHORity (Credibility) and Collaborative Contribution so that you can maximize your efforts to raise your value in the marketplace, allowing you to increase the cost for your services. Most importantly, Lane has the unparalleled ability to take your story and help you turn it into a signature keynote.

He teaches you the skills to empower others and leverage your uniqueness for captivating new prospects and acquiring new clients. As a 2x #1 bestselling author he turns you from an author to an AUTHORity! Together, we will help define your lane, build your overall brand to monetize most effectively and increase the size of your digital footprint to maximize your global reach and impact.

Haris Reis is the President &
COO of Changing Lanes
International. He is also a
National Award Winning
Entrepreneur, #1 National
Best-Selling Author,
Keynote Speaker and Elite
Marketing Consultant.

He has helped Changing
Lanes International become
a 6-figure business in a year.
He was previously a growth
hacker at VaynerMedia
building Gary Vaynerchuk's
personal brand and ran paid
media for the top 1% users
on Facebook. The videos he
has created have been
shared with people that
have over 130k followers,
has been in videos that collectively reached over 1.5 million
people, created videos that cumulatively received over 4.4
million views, and has produced nearly $100k in sales for
products/services over the phone.

He has been featured in The Young Entrepreneurs podcast,
College Startup, Collegiate Entrepreneurs' Organization,
Live Out Loud, Experts Showcase, The Ambitious Life
Magazine and the Life Leveraging Series.

Haris has a passion for helping business owners develop
products/services as well as creating the digital marketing
to promote the products/services. He loves running paid
media and building funnels that automate businesses while
keeping a personal touch. He has also helped build a social
media following to bricks & mortar businesses
internationally. His passion is helping you get your voice
and message out to the world through marketing.

Connect with Lane & Haris

Lane@changinglanesinternational.com

Haris@changinglanesinternational.com